Bananas

·AN·
AMERICAN
HISTORY

VIRGINIA SCOTT JENKINS

SMITHSONIAN INSTITUTION PRESS

WASHINGTON AND LONDON

EDITOR: Ruth W. Spiegel
DESIGNER: Amber Frid-Jimenez

Library of Congress Cataloging-in-Publication Data
Jenkins, Virginia Scott.
Bananas: an American history / Virginia S. Jenkins.
p.   cm.
Includes bibliographical references and index.
ISBN 1-56098-966-1 (alk. paper)
1. Banana trade—United States–History.
2. Bananas–Social aspects—-United States.
I. Title.
HD9259.B3 U537 2000
380.1'414772'0973—dc21   00-027403

British Library Cataloguing-in-Publication Data available

Manufactured in the United States of America
07 06 05 04 03 02 01 00   5 4 3 2 1

♾ The recycled paper used in this publication meets the minimum re-
quirements of the American National Standard for Information
Sciences—Permanence of Paper for Printed Library Materials ANSI
Z39.48-1984.

Except for photographs 1, 5, 30, and 32, all photography is by Virginia
Scott Jenkins; these four photographs are courtesy of the Winterthur
Museum, Winterthur, Delaware. Except for the same photographs and
28 and 29, all photographs are courtesy of Ann Lovell's Banana
Museum, Auburn, Washington. For permission to reproduce any of the
illustrations, please correspond directly with the owners of the works.
The Smithsonian Institution Press does not retain reproduction rights
for these illustrations individually, or maintain a file of addresses for
photo sources.

CONTENTS

ACKNOWLEDGMENTS

I wish to thank the Winterthur Library for a one-month appointment as a Research Fellow and the opportunity to explore the use of bananas in nineteenth-century American art, cookbooks, and etiquette manuals. Ann Lovell's Banana Museum in Auburn, Washington, has been a wonderful resource and I am thankful for her continued interest and for allowing me to disrupt the museum to take photographs for this book. Thanks to all my friends, family, and students who contributed banana jokes, advertisements, and enough banana stuff to start my own museum. I also want to thank Thomas Anastasio and Sally Levy who read and commented on the book in various drafts. I am grateful to my husband and to Musa, the sailor dog, for their love and patient support during the course of this project.

INTRODUCTION

The field of food studies is growing as more scholars become interested in the historical, social, and cultural meanings of food. Historians, philosophers, folklorists, and literary scholars are turning to the once-mundane topic of food to study human nature and specific cultures by the way people gather, cook, eat, market, and talk about food. Food can be a symbol of power, an aesthetic display, a community ritual, or an expression of ideology or identity. The study of food can provide a window into issues of gender, class, race, and ethnicity.[1] Food and its attendant meanings provide the basis for many of our daily actions, for wars of conquest and trade, for political conflicts, and for the identification of the foreigner, the "other."

A study of the banana at first may appear frivolous, but the social history of the use of everyday food can offer a window into the culture of the United States in the late nineteenth and twentieth centuries. "When unfamiliar substances are taken up by new users, they enter into pre-existing social and psychological contexts and acquire—or are given—contextual meanings by those who use them."[2] This study is a look at the context of the banana in the United States, a way to elicit meanings from the ways bananas have been absorbed into popular culture, to explain ourselves, our politics, culture, fears, and dreams.

The first Boy Scout *Handbook*, published in 1911, supplied a list of good deeds that a boy might do each day, including chopping wood for mother's stove, helping an old lady across the street, and picking banana peels up off the sidewalk. Why were banana peels mentioned specifically rather than litter or garbage in general? How many peels were there? Who was dropping them? Was this really a problem? What was going on in 1911 on our city streets?

I remember several instances from my childhood that may have piqued my own interest in bananas. When I was about nine years old, I read all the Lucy Fitch Perkins books I could find about twins in various countries and historical settings. *The Filipino Twins* family lived in a thatched-roof house on stilts and it was the job of the boy twin to polish the floor using banana leaves.[3] I actually remembered it as banana skins that he used to skate on around the floor and only discovered years later that it was the leaves. This sounded like a wonderful way to do housecleaning and fit into my American perceptions of the slippery properties of the banana peel.

About the same time, I was entranced by a banana stalk hanging in a neighborhood grocery store window. It had a single hand of bananas left on it and I wanted that stalk. It took me some time to gather enough courage to enter the store and ask for it, but once I had the stalk in hand, oh, it was a thing of wonder. With it I could conjure up images of jungles and foreign travel. To me, bananas represented exotic, mysterious, romantic places.

Then there's the third banana memory. It is a recipe that my mother may have gotten from the *New York Times Magazine* of September 14, 1947, for bananas spread with mustard, rolled in a ham slice secured with toothpicks, and baked in cheese sauce.[4] This dish made an occasional appearance on the family dinner table. It was the only thing I ever cooked that my husband refused to eat.

Questions of where, when, and how bananas are eaten illustrate changes in diet, eating habits, and etiquette. Bananas have been instrumental in public health campaigns for clean streets and tuberculosis control. International fruit companies were leaders in the development of modern advertising and marketing strategies. They stimulated trade and political relations between the United States and the countries of the Caribbean and laid the basis for the development of modern multinational corporations. The story of the banana illustrates aspects of the development of our national transportation system, including railroads, steamships, and trucking. Banana jokes, songs, and symbolism also allow us to look at our changing mores and concerns.

Before the 1880s, most Americans had never seen, much less eaten, a banana but by 1910 the country was flooded with them. Transformed from a luxury and a novelty, bananas had become the poor man's fruit. In that year it was estimated that three billion bananas were imported into the United States—"a shipment which would cover an area twenty feet wide reaching from New York to San Francisco, or, placed end to end, would extend thirteen times around the Earth at the Equator."[5]

Throughout most of the twentieth century, residents of the United States have eaten more pounds of bananas per capita than any other fruit. Unlike kiwi fruit or mangoes, bananas quickly lost the allure of the exotic. Thanks to early marketing decisions by United Fruit, bananas are perceived as always available and always cheap. In 1995 Americans spent over $3.4 billion on imported bananas: a banana a week for every person in the country.[6] By 1999 annual consumption had risen to seventy-five bananas per person, or a banana and a half a week.[7] That is over twenty-seven and a half pounds of bananas per person each year, nine pounds more than our annual consumption of apples, the next most popular fruit.[8] Bananas have become as "American" as apples or strawberries despite the fact that virtually all our bananas are imported from the countries of the Caribbean basin.

Bananas have become ubiquitous, truly a part of our lives for the past hundred years. Bananas are so common that they are almost invisible. Few supermarket shoppers think about where the bananas came from. In the 1990s we got 60 percent of our winter vegetables

"Banana," Artemas Ward, *Grocers' Hand-Book and Directory for 1886.*

from Mexico, and are so used to the availability of foreign fruits and vegetables that we seldom think about their origin. Bananas are our friends—ordinary, funny, homey. By looking closely at the banana, we can learn a great deal about our way of life, our trade and transport systems, and our politics. As the banana quickly changed from a luxury to the cheapest fruit available, it found an enduring niche in American humor and folklore. Bananas are part of our national cuisine, and they also appear in popular songs, jokes, vaudeville acts, and films. We have eaten them for a wide variety of healthful reasons and some have even tried to smoke the peels. This book is about the importance of bananas in American culture and the meanings that bananas have assumed for us.

The first chapter traces the introduction of bananas to the United States in the nineteenth century. There are unauthenticated reports that a shipment of bananas reached Salem, Massachusetts, in 1690 and that the New Englanders boiled the fruit with pork and promptly gave up in disgust.[9] It would be another hundred and fifty years before the next report of bananas in East Coast ports. Visitors to the Philadelphia Centennial Exposition in 1876 could purchase their first banana, wrapped in tinfoil, for ten cents, a high price in those days. It would be another twenty years before bananas were widely available.

The second chapter traces the development of the major American banana-importing companies, the original multinational corporations of the twentieth century. Several enterprising American ship captains recognized that there was a market for bananas, and began to encourage the people of the Caribbean to grow enough for export, as well as undertaking the risky business of shipping bananas to East Coast ports. As these fruit companies diversified, grew, and merged, they lost their original identities in huge multinational conglomerates.

Chapter 3 explores the growth of our modern transportation system using the banana as an example of a perishable commodity that was difficult to move from producer to consumer. Steamships, refrigeration, packaging, railroads, and trucking all have played an important role in the banana business, often inspiring modifications and new inventions to handle the fruit and to meet the demands of the grocer and the consumer.

Chapter 4 is about marketing, the business of selling bananas to the customer. In Boston, United Fruit decided on a policy that was to change America's eating habits. Bananas would be marketed as cheaply as possible—as the poor man's fruit.

Chapter 5 looks at public health and sanitation issues in connection with the popularization of the banana. The banana made its appearance in the United States at the time when Americans first were learning about germs, vitamins, and calories. The issues of immigration, street cleaning, nutrition, and the fight against tuberculosis all contained a banana motif. Bananas were advertised as the fruit in the germ-proof wrapper to assuage fears of food contamination. In addition, bananas were touted as an almost complete food, full of vitamins, minerals, and carbohydrates.

The sixth chapter takes a closer look at the consumption of bananas. In the nineteenth century, bananas were eaten in the United States on special occasions such as Christmas and elegant christening parties. In the twentieth century, banana splits and banana bread have become ubiquitous, and almost all of us slice bananas onto our breakfast cereal. Researchers have found ways to preserve, powder, and distill bananas so that many new banana-flavored products have found their way onto supermarket shelves since 1990.

Chapter 7 is devoted to the twin cities of Fulton, Kentucky, and South Fulton, Tennessee. These places were called the Banana Capital of the World in the 1960s when the community began to celebrate their connections with Central America. The Fulton Annual International Banana Festival was held for over thirty years, despite the fact that banana trains from New Orleans ceased stopping in Fulton for inspection in the early 1970s.

Finally there's a look at how bananas have become rooted in American life despite the fact that they have never been a selection of the Fruit of the Month Club.[10] Their place in American culture is very much like that of the hot dog. Almost everyone likes bananas, but no one takes them seriously. Bananas appear in songs, films, and jokes. Everyone knows the danger of slipping on a banana peel. Bananas are funny, sexy, kitsch, and smoking banana peels was once considered cool. Bananas also represent romance, the tropics, and adventure. The last chapter explores the many meanings ascribed to bananas in American culture.

1

INTRODUCING

Bananas

THE BANANA IS ANY OF A VARIETY of tropical or subtropical plants of the genus *Musa* (possibly from *Muz*, Arabic for banana) that bear clusters of long yellow or reddish fruits. There are sixty-seven species and more than two hundred varieties of *Musa*.[1] Bananas may have been cultivated as early as 1000 B.C. in the rain forests of Southeast Asia. Arabs brought the fruit to the Middle East and Africa in the seventh century. In 1482 the Portuguese found bananas growing as a staple food on Africa's west coast in what is now Gambia, Sierra Leone, and Liberia, and transplanted them to the Canary Islands.[2]

The botanical name of the type of banana familiar to grocery shoppers in the United States, *Musa sapientum,* means "fruit of the wise men." It was so named by the eighteenth-century Swedish botanist Linnaeus because the Roman historian Pliny (A.D. 23–79) wrote that the sages of India rested in the shade of the plant and ate its fruit.[3] The word banana was first printed in English in the seventeenth century.[4]

Linnaeus named the related plantain *Musa paradisiaca* or "heavenly fruit" because of a legend that it, not the apple, was the forbidden fruit of Paradise.[5] In a variety of West African languages the

"The Banana Family," *Story of the Banana,* Education
Department, United Fruit, Boston, 1936.

fruit Musa is known as "banna," "bana," "gbana," "abana," "funana,"
and "banane."

Plantains are starchy and thick-skinned bananas that are used
mostly for cooking, while the everyday bananas imported into the
United States are usually eaten raw. The flesh of plantains is salmon-
colored when ripe and cooked, and tastes different at each stage of
its development.[6] Plantains are integral to the diet of Africa and

Latin America, cooked the same ways as potatoes, but until recently have not been imported in large quantities or found in grocery stores in many parts of the United States. They have never been marketed on the grand scale of bananas, and for that reason have not been included in this book's exploration of bananas' effect on mainstream culture.

There is no evidence that bananas grew in the Western Hemisphere before the voyages of Columbus, and the Spanish are credited with bringing bananas to the New World from the Canary Islands. In 1516 Friar Tomas de Berlanga, a Catholic missionary priest of the Order of Predicadores, landed on the Island of Hispaniola (now Haiti and the Dominican Republic) and planted banana stems or rhizomes as the cheapest and most satisfactory food for the growing African slave population. When Friar Tomas was made Bishop of Panama, he took banana plants with him to the mainland.[7] Vasco de Quiroga, first bishop of Michoácan, is said to have introduced bananas to Mexico.[8] The plants spread rapidly throughout Central America, Mexico, and southern Florida, so much so that later observers believed the banana to be native to this continent.[9] The first English colonists of Roanoke, Virginia, took banana stocks with them from the Caribbean islands to plant in a decidedly nontropical climate.[10]

Bananas do not grow on trees; in fact, the banana is a huge herbaceous plant that grows to a height of fifteen to thirty feet. It is perhaps the largest plant on earth that does not have a woody stem above the ground.[11] This makes it susceptible to wind-storm damage. The plants grow from rhizomes that have buds or "eyes" like a potato, and new plants grow up from shoots around the parent stalk. The rhizomes can be separated and transplanted to establish new plants.[12] The commercial bananas familiar to most Americans have three sets of chromosomes instead of the usual two, which causes the fruit to be large, hardy, and seedless. The tiny dark specks in the center of a banana are the infertile vestigial seeds. Diploid bananas, with two sets of chromosomes, do contain numbers of hard seeds, some as big as half a pencil eraser.[13]

About Bananas, Education Department, United
Fruit, Boston, 1936.

Commercially grown bananas are planted in rows "very much like
hills of corn except, of course, at a greater distance apart."[14] Planting can be spaced in a plantation so that fruit is continuously coming to maturity. As the plants develop, they produce a red flower
that points downward toward the ground. Eventually the bracts
drop off, exposing the young bananas that originate from the clusters of flowers arranged spirally around the stalk. As the fruits develop they bend upward so that they end by pointing toward the sky.

The fruit grows on a single stalk with seven to ten bunches each holding twelve to fourteen individual fruits. Bunches are known as "hands," and the individual fruits are called "fingers."

It takes about eighteen months for the banana plant to grow from a shoot to produce a mature bunch of fruit.[15] The stalks, each containing up to 150 individual bananas, generally weigh from eighty to a hundred pounds. Bananas are usually cut green, even in the tropics, since they tend to toughen, sour, and split open, attracting insects, if allowed to ripen on the plant. Each plant fruits only once; when the plant has produced its fruit, it is cut down and left to decay to form humus that supports another shoot growing from the same stem.

To bear fruit, a banana plant needs from 14 to 23 consecutive months of frost-free, sunny weather. Although they can be grown in Florida, Louisiana, Texas, and even parts of California, bananas are not viable as a commercial crop in the continental United States

"Banana Plants of Three, Six, and Nine Months' Growth,"
Story of the Banana, United Fruit, Boston, 1925, 24.

north of 30° latitude where the temperature normally falls below 50 degrees F.[16] In the far south and in greenhouses, the plants will fruit but not consistently enough to sustain large-scale commercial planting.[17] A 1904 publication noted that "while bananas can be grown as far north as Florida, to reach their perfection a much warmer climate is needed and a much larger rainfall. Cuba is too far north to produce the very best results."[18] Bananas are popular as ornamental plants both indoors and out in many parts of the country, but when night-time temperatures dip below 60°F, it is time to bring the plants indoors.

Banana plants were probably planted in Spanish settlements in southern Florida, where Cavendish bananas were found growing as a dooryard plant in the nineteenth century.[19] There have been sporadic efforts since to foster commercial banana farming in Florida in response to the enormous profits in banana importing and the growth of the North American market. The U.S. Department of Agriculture introduced Chinese dwarf cooking-bananas to Florida in 1841 but there was little interest among consumers at that time.[20]

A Colonel Whitner was reported to have ten thousand banana plants growing on his plantation near Silver Lake, Florida, in 1876. An observer noted that "some of these are large trees, which do not die after bearing their fruit, but the majority are of the dwarf species, which are renewed every year."[21] The January 1879 "Sunday School Leaflet of the American Home Missionary Society" listed bananas among the exotic fruit to be found in Florida, while a tourist guide to Florida published in 1891 listed bananas as a "staple commodity capable of being raised in Florida and shipped to outside markets with a profit to the producer."[22] This and other efforts to promote banana growing in Florida have consistently failed because of periodic frosts that can devastate entire plantations.

In 1913 a British publication noted that banana plants could be found in the United States along the coast of the Gulf of Mexico "although fruit is not expected more than once in four or five years" owing to periodic frosts. The report stated that in southern Florida "there are few large patches, though nearly everyone has a few plants. The fruit is generally inferior in quality, as compared with tropical fruit." The author believed that there was little commercial cultivation of bananas because "the fruit can be grown so much more cheaply in Central America and the West Indies."[23]

In 1921 W. E. Bolles of Oldsmar, Florida, organized the Florida Banana-Growers Association to try to grow bananas on a commercial scale.[24] Bolles saw an enormous market for Florida bananas sold at the same wholesale prices as imported fruit, as much as "$1,400 per acre per year, when they get going good."[25] No one came to the first meeting, twenty people attended the second meeting, and over two hundred attended the annual association meeting in October 1923.[26]

The 1920s' Florida land speculation boom, fueled by eastern investors, may have had something to do with this sudden interest in banana farming, and growers reported making more per acre from bananas than from oranges and grapefruit. Soon an estimated two thousand acres were planted to bananas.[27] Bolles believed that "there are reasonable probabilities of growing bananas commercially not only in all Florida, but in southern Louisiana and southern Texas, and the plant can be made to fruit in southern Georgia and California."[28]

A U.S. Department of Agriculture report on banana growing in Florida was more cautious. In the midst of the land speculation boom, the report noted that "there is nothing to justify the expectation that the crop will be profitable on land purchased at inflated or speculative prices even when climatic and soil factors are favorable." The report warned:

Ownership of small tracts forming a part of a large planting managed as a unit is sometimes featured as a promising method of promoting banana culture and on a commercial scale in Florida. Non-residents are in many cases induced to become investors in such projects, influenced by statements showing large prospective profits, comparable to some of the banana-

growing enterprises in tropical America. Such statements usually presuppose almost ideal growing and marketing conditions,
of which growers in the continental United States are not assured. Before making such investments a personal inspection of
the site is in all cases desirable. Claims made with regard to
prospective earnings should be weighed by the same standards
that would be applied to other lines of production in which the
owner's personal interest and supervision are usually necessary
to profitable operation.[29]

Interest continued in commercial banana growing but the reality of
the climate, and the price of land and labor combined to make
U.S.–grown bananas uncompetitive with those imported from Central America. A USDA report written in 1934 noted that "any commercial planting to be successful over a long period should not only
be made in a warm location, but some sort of artificial protection
against cold injury should be provided either by the use of wood
fires (commonly used in Florida citrus groves) or by the use of some
form of orchard heater."[30] A report issued by the Association of
American Railroads in 1946 noted that "efforts to cultivate bananas
commercially in the United States have been unsuccessful," and
that there was "an insignificant (and probably experimental) domestic production of bananas in Florida."[31]

In 1952 the Florida Department of Agriculture published a report on banana growing that followed the same lines as the
reports in the 1920s, with the rueful conclusion that "the one great
difficulty in growing bananas in Florida is the rather general in-
scrutability of our climatic conditions to most varieties."[32] The big
American banana-growing and -importing companies concentrated
their efforts in the Caribbean basin, leaving the risky Florida business to growers who sold their bananas on the local market or to
tourists from roadside stands.[33]

Bananas grew on the Hawaiian Islands when the islands were visited by Capt. James Cook in 1799.[34] The *Hawaiian Almanac and Annual for 1891* listed bananas as an export crop, beginning with 121

bunches in 1862. Exports gradually increased to 105,630 bunches in 1889.[35] These records do not specify where the bananas were being shipped. In 1901 the U.S. Department of Agriculture established an Agricultural Experiment Station in Hawaii that from the start paid a great deal of attention to bananas, researchers finding a dozen varieties with commercial possibilities.[36] By 1926, with the development of modern shipping facilities, commercial production increased to about 200,000 bunches annually.[37] Twenty years later, bananas received on the United States mainland from Hawaii and Puerto Rico combined amounted to less than 1 percent of total banana imports.[38] Today the continental American banana market continues to be supplied by the countries of Central America. The state of Hawaii has never had a significant commercial banana industry.[39]

As an aside, in the United States there is only one successful commercial banana-growing business. In the 1980s Doug Richardson and Paul Turner began growing bananas in an unusual ecological niche on the California coast. Seaside Banana Gardens in La Conchita, 75 miles north of Los Angeles, lies on a narrow crescent of land backed by 300-foot-high bluffs. The ocean on one side keeps the temperature constant, the bluffs protect the plants from wind, the sun streams across the land all day long, and the area has proven itself perfect for banana-growing. Richardson and Turner planted fifty-five varieties of bananas (2,500 plants) and developed a successful organic banana business with clients across the country. The varieties grown at Seaside Banana Gardens included the Brazilian ladyfinger, the apple banana, the Hawaiian Popoulu, and a group of Polynesian cooking varieties.[40]

Residents of the United States became familiar with bananas in a variety of ways. Missionary society Sunday school stories about exotic tropical places included tales of bananas and other strange fruit; the Philadelphia Centennial Exposition featured tropical plants including the banana; cookbooks, newspaper articles, and advertisements promoted the new fruit. Bananas began to appear in retail networks, in greengrocer shops, and on pushcarts. They were linked to romantic adventure and associated with palm trees, warm weather, and perpetual vacation.

Many nineteenth-century writers confused the banana and the plantain.[41] One described the banana as "similar in composition to the potato. In some tropical countries it is much used as a food, especially in Cuba, where the negroes make a sort of ragout, of which the banana is the principal ingredient."[42] This was probably a description of the plantain. *A Domestic Cyclopaedia of Practical Information* (1877) made no distinction between the banana and the plantain:

BANANA. The fruit of the palm tree [*sic*], found in the West Indies and South America, and throughout the tropical regions of both hemispheres. In the countries where it grows it is almost always the staple food, occupying the same place there as the cereals with us. No other product of the vegetable kingdom affords so much nutriment from a given space of ground as the banana, and no other food is so peculiarly adapted to support life in the tropics. It is estimated that a quarter of an acre planted in bananas will produce enough for a family of five the year round. It grows in thick clusters of 150 to 200 to the cluster. It is eaten raw, either alone or cut in slices with sugar and cream, or wine and orange juice. It is also roasted, fried or boiled, and is made into fritters, preserves, and marmalades. It is dried in the sun and preserved as figs; meal is extracted from it by pounding and made into something resembling bread; and the fermented juice affords an excellent wine. With us it is brought to the table as dessert, and proved universally acceptable. The best kind, when they can be procured fresh, are the "lady-fingers" as they are called. They are found in our markets from March to October.[43]

In 1872 housewives were told that "bananas have a taste something like muskmelons. They are not improved by cooking, yet may be preserved to taste as well as when raw. Boil them two or three minutes in a little water, with a teaspoon of sugar to each banana, and bottle; or put them raw in a bottle, fill it with boiling water, and seal."[44]

Bananas were also described as being "as large as a cucumber and resembling it in color and shape. This fruit is filled with a sweet nutritious custard-like juice, and is eaten raw, boiled, baked, and cooked in various ways. It is preserved with sugar and with vinegar; is used as bread; and when pressed and fermented yields a spirituous drink resembling cider. The sap also makes an excellent wine."[45] These authors may have assumed that the exotic fruit could be used as other fruits without themselves testing the recipes. They knew of bananas but do not themselves appear to have been familiar with them.

In the nineteenth century the people of the United States loved fruit and enjoyed many varieties of domestic fruits and berries. They had also enthusiastically adopted such exotic imported delicacies as the pineapple and the coconut. But some Americans were wary of imported fruit. The author of *The Young Housekeeper* wrote: "Were our foreign imported aliments perfect in their kinds—fruits among the rest—I should have less objection to their use than I now have. But it does seem to me very unreasonable to use imperfect, unripe, dried or half-decayed substances, merely because they came across the water, in preference to our equally rich and more perfect domestic productions."[46]

The Centennial Exposition in Philadelphia in 1876 included a forty-acre display of tropical plants in the Horticultural Hall with orange trees, a banana plant, date palms, wax plants, century plants, sago palms, fig trees, orchids, and pineapples.[47] The banana plant was so popular that a guard had to be posted near it so that visitors would not pull it apart for souvenirs. The New York Flower Show in 1890 also featured banana plants that attracted considerable interest "for their application to domestic and commercial economy."[48]

Many American children became familiar with pictures of banana "trees" in school textbooks and Sunday school books, and learned the pleasing but "inaccurate information that the fortunate natives of the tropics have nothing to do but roam the flowery glades and live on bananas."[49] Between 1860 and 1890, missionary reports from Jamaica, Mexico, and South America often included descriptions of bananas as part of the exotic setting.[50]

Bananas were available at a specialty greengrocer in Philadelphia in 1876, wrapped in tinfoil at 10 cents apiece—an hour's wage for many people. (At that time, tinfoil was also used to preserve lemons, chocolate, and tobacco.[51]) One young visitor to the Centennial Exposition remembered the excitement when his father bought half a dozen bananas to take back to their hotel room for a feast. The father, familiar with bananas from travels in the Caribbean, was disappointed in the quality of the fruit, but the boy was thrilled and took a peel home with him to show his friends back in Illinois. By the time he got there, the peel had blackened and shriveled and he was disappointed that his friends were not suitably impressed. It was not until the mid-1880s that people in the Midwest became somewhat familiar with the banana as a fruit and could find them in grocery stores. Even then bananas were expensive and remained a luxury item for some time.[52]

Fruit still-life paintings were popular throughout the nineteenth century as appropriate pictures to hang in dining rooms. These paintings reflected the prosperity of the times, with lush fruit and flower displays and depictions of dessert tables set with fine crystal, silver, and linen.[53] These still-life paintings carried a variety of symbolic meanings, representing abundance, fertility, and the riches of America. It is interesting that bananas were a relatively rare subject for still-life painters.[54] Pineapples—another tropical, imported fruit—were used more frequently, symbolic of hospitality. A few paintings included a single banana, perhaps an indication of the rarity or cost of the fruit.[55] Most of these pictures represented local, seasonal fruits and nuts that perhaps were considered more patriotic than images of foreign fruits.

For those who could not afford an original oil painting, after the Civil War there were still-life lithographs by Currier and Ives, Louis Prang, and many other American lithographers.[56] Louis Prang's chromolithographs were extremely popular and reflected popular taste. Jay Gould and others also published chromolithographs that included a number of still-life dining room pictures, but there is no indication in their catalogs that bananas were included in the subject matter.[57]

Young ladies in the Victorian era learned to model and paint wax fruit and flowers and to decorate their dining rooms with wax fruit arrangements. One manual noted that "in a basket of fruit, lady apples are beautiful, crab apples, Seckel pears, Bartlett pears, a lemon, an orange or two, California plums, two peaches, and grapes are desirable. Two pounds of wax will make this elegant variety."[58] Bananas were not included in such instructions, perhaps because the form was considered indelicate or inappropriate for young women to make.

As bananas became more familiar, less expensive, and more widely available, inhibitions about using bananas as decorative motifs in the dining room apparently disappeared. By the mid-1880s, bananas were being included in table centerpiece arrangements of fresh fruit and flowers. Readers of *The Cook* were instructed that "fruit should always make the centre display on the luncheon table. The variety is so large at present, red and yellow bananas, oranges, peaches, apricots, cherries, and grapes, that with a little taste, a very attractive pyramid may be formed."[59] Bananas may have been irresistible for their shape and the bright yellow and red colors for those attempting to create stable pyramid centerpieces. The fruit could be arranged using a large flat dish with a tumbler in the center to give the fruit some height, draped with ferns or moss. A pineapple might be placed on top of the tumbler, and then oranges, bananas, pears, two or three colors of grapes, and plums be arranged around it. Beginners were warned that "the dish must look light and rather carelessly arranged, but the fruit must be placed that there shall be no danger of its falling."[60] Fruit might also grace the breakfast table and, readers were admonished "should be your table decoration instead of flowers, which refined taste begins to find out of place among meats and vegetables."[61]

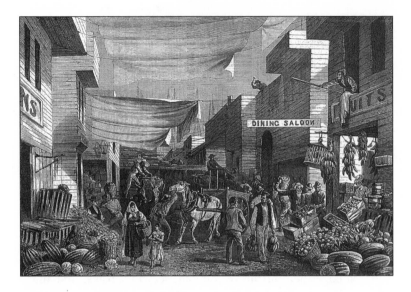

"Bananas at the Washington Market," New York, *Harper's Weekly*,
September 14, 1878, 737.

By the mid-1880s, housewives could find red and yellow bananas
in the East Coast ports of New York, Philadelphia, and Boston. In
addition, fig bananas and plantains were generally available in
New York and Philadelphia. Fig bananas were described as "small,
golden yellow and very sweet. They are simply delicious."[62] Readers
of *The Cook: A Weekly Handbook of Domestic Culinary Art for All Housekeepers* learned that

> there are a number of different kinds of bananas grown in the
> tropics, but the choicest are seldom or never brought to New
> York; first, because the lazy and ignorant people who live where
> the bananas grow do not take any trouble to cultivate enough
> of the best kinds to make their shipment anything of a business;
> second, because the fine bananas are too delicate for long
> transportation. The "strawberry" and "apple" varieties are the
> choicest; the "fig" next."[63]

Despite the many delicious varieties of banana, American fruit importers first concentrated on the Gros Michel (Big Mike), and later the Cavendish, because they were large and easy to ship. Both varieties have thick skins that do not bruise easily. Another important factor in the decision to concentrate on these two varieties was that all the fingers on these stalks ripen at once, about three weeks after they are harvested, making them easier to handle.[64]

Bananas were familiar to many Americans by the end of the nineteenth century, although as late as 1899 an article in *Scientific American* included directions for peeling them ("the fruit is peeled by slitting the skin longitudinally and giving it a rotary motion with the hands").[65] Bananas were available in many parts of the country, although still expensive and considered a luxury outside the port cities on the East Coast. Fruit-importing companies knew they had a profitable item if they could only procure a consistent supply of the fruit abroad and expand their markets at home.

Just six years later, in 1905, an article on bananas in *Scientific American* pointed out that "only a few years ago the banana was a luxury in many northern families. Although fairly common on the city markets, it was too expensive to be generally used by most families living in and near the small towns; but now so abundant and cheap as to be a common article of commerce in every corner grocery store, while in the cities it is frequently referred to as the poor man's fruit."[66] The twentieth century was to see a phenomenal growth in the banana-importing industry with the rise of giant multinational corporations. Bananas became the cheapest fruit in the grocery store throughout the year, taken for granted by consumers. The banana lost its exotic image and disappeared from the formal dinner table as it became the most widely eaten fruit in the United States.

2

POLITICS AND

Bananas

THE TREMENDOUS GROWTH OF THE United States after the Civil War stimulated foreign trade and made capital available for overseas investment. Americans were hungry for more space, more land, more markets, more resources. Foreign trade was a symbol of national power. The navy and foreign service expanded to protect the lucrative businesses, while many citizens called for more colonies and a more activist foreign policy. Expanding rapidly in the late nineteenth century, American cities became centers of foreign commerce and cosmopolitan culture.

Many Americans believed that selling, buying, and investing in foreign markets was critical to the economic health and development of the country. They reasoned that the problems of overproduction and unemployment that led to the depression of the 1890s could be relieved by opening foreign markets to American agricultural surplus and manufactured goods.

Several entrepreneurs in the transportation business experimented with importing tropical products such as fruit and lumber. One problem they faced was the cultivation of an adequate and steady supply of these products for exportation in areas lacking the necessary workforce and the infrastructure of roads, railroads, harbors, and port facilities. In the 1870s Charles Frank (or Carl Franc), a Pacific Mail Steamship Line steward, began to develop banana plantations in Panama. In the 1880s Lorenzo Dow Baker, a Cape Cod fishing captain, in partnership with Andrew Preston, a Boston produce agent, established a market for bananas in Boston and laid the foundation for the United Fruit Company. Baker encouraged banana growing in Jamaica by carrying bananas on his return voyages to New England markets. Others, like Santo Oteri and Salvador D'Antoni, sailed schooners loaded with bananas from Honduras to New Orleans.[1] In 1900 D'Antoni and the Vaccaro family in New Orleans created the Standard Fruit and Steamship Company. The Standard Fruit and United Fruit companies came to dominate the American banana markets during the first half of the twentieth century.

The growing popularity of bananas in the United States pushed entrepreneurs to expand banana production in Central America and the Caribbean islands as well as to search for ways to grow bananas at home. Producers experimented with banana plant products in an effort to exploit the new resource fully.

Scientific American, in 1896, suggested that "almost every part of the plant can be used for some useful purpose: the stalk forms an excellent material for the manufacture of paper, or the fiber might be extracted; the peel of the fruit will make excellent indelible ink; the green fruit dried can be converted into wholesome flour."[2] The author suggested that "green bananas, boiled tender, if given to the hens cut up, will make them lay more eggs than any other food." An article in *Harper's Weekly* that same year suggested that the shoots of the banana plant could be cooked as greens, and that "its stalk yields a valuable fibre which is woven into textile fabrics, twisted into rope, and manufactured into paper."[3]

The lust for colonies and imperial adventure fueled the Spanish American War in 1898. This in turn opened the banana market wider for American companies. An 1899 article in *Scientific American*, with the title "The Banana as the Basis of a New Industry," noted that "the banana grows well in our new possessions in the

West Indies, and we have no lack of delicious fruit which has great food value as well. Unfortunately, however, bananas do not stand long sea voyages, and the result is that a considerable market is closed to them."[4] This situation did not last long as steamships were quickly replacing sailing schooners in the Caribbean trade.

American fruit companies taught Americans to eat bananas at the same time as they encouraged the people of the Caribbean basin to grow bananas on a commercial basis. Local banana growers in Jamaica, Cuba, and elsewhere expanded their cultivation of banana plants in response to the increasing North American demand for the fruit. Many independent growers were able to profit with very small investment.

Once the demand for bananas had become firmly established, fruit-importing companies found that in order to remain competitive they had to invest in land, in more and bigger refrigerated ships, and in adequate storage and loading facilities in Central American ports. As banana cultivation spread inland, transportation systems including railway networks and deep-water ports were designed and built. U.S.-based companies such as United Fruit and Standard Fruit negotiated land concessions, tax exemptions, use of other natural resources, and free import of numerous products with the host governments of the Central American banana-growing countries.[5] In the process, most small-scale local producers were either absorbed or forced out of business.

Much of the suitable banana-growing land was found in sparsely populated Caribbean lowland. This meant that U.S. companies had to import a labor force, construct company towns, provide stores, hospitals, and schools, construct telegraph and telephone systems, and generally build the entire infrastructure for a modern community. Indigenous people, displaced from their jungle lands and ways of life, were hired as low-wage laborers on the new agricultural factory plantations. They were joined by many Jamaican and East Indian men, hired to work on the Panama Canal, who migrated to the central American mainland banana plantations when the canal was finished. This markedly changed the ethnic makeup and social structure of Central America.

At first, much like the American West, Central America appeared to have limitless resources. For many Americans, it was the new frontier. The fruit companies concentrated on increasing worker productivity in the face of a limited local labor pool and problems of importing labor from the Caribbean islands, the East Indies, and the United States. Technical innovations included railroads, overhead conveyor systems, steamships, deepwater piers, and eventually on-site boxing of the fruit. The constant push to modernize, industrialize, and streamline production was an effort to keep down costs and avoid unionization among the workers.

The United States acquired few colonies in the Caribbean and Central America, but was able to develop an informal empire based on economic and political control rather than by formal annexation. By 1914 investments by U.S. citizens in Latin America amounted to $1.26 billion. American exports to Latin America exceeded $300 million, and imports from Latin America had increased even more. Between 1900 and 1917, American troops intervened in Cuba, Panama, Nicaragua, the Dominican Republic, Mexico, and Haiti to protect United States investments and businesses. North American companies controlled the tariff revenues and budgets of these countries, renegotiated foreign debts with American banks, trained national guards, and ran elections. Investments in sugar, tobacco, transportation, and banking were most apparent, but the banana business was a lead player in the international game.

Banana-growing enclave economies came to be a central feature of many of the countries of the Caribbean basin.[6] The banana business had little direct effect on the national economies as a whole, since the economic result was limited to the banana-plantation zones.[7] Workers spent their wages in company stores while supplies and equipment were imported by the company rather than purchased within the country or region. The banana plantations had very little direct impact on the manufacturing and retail life of the host country. Bananas and coffee often accounted for 80 percent of the exports of Central American countries but the economic benefits were limited to members of the governments in power. Often the United States companies had managed to acquire so many concessions in taxes and importing rights that very little banana revenue remained in the country where the fruit was grown. The term "banana republic" was coined around 1935 to describe a corrupt and hopeless puppet dictatorship in a country whose government was unduly influenced by United Fruit and other American fruit-exporting companies.[8]

As North American corporations operating in Latin America grew in size and power, many were accused of economic imperialism. United Fruit Company was the chief target and was known to many as El Pulpo, the Octopus. By 1927 United Fruit operations had expanded to include the production and transportation of a variety of tropical products, including about half the bananas consumed in the United States.[9] In 1930 United Fruit owned 63 percent of the 103 million bunches of bananas imported.[10] In 1946 the company owned 465,000 acres of improved land—of which 130,000 acres were planted to bananas—in Cuba, Jamaica, Guatemala, Honduras, Nicaragua, Costa Rica, Panama, Colombia, and the Dominican Republic.[11]

Standard Fruit was United Fruit's strongest competitor. It was begun in 1899 when four Sicilian immigrants (the brothers Joseph, Luca, and Felix Vaccaro, and Salvador D'Antoni) who lived in New Orleans started importing bananas. They chartered a 188-ton British steamship, *Premier,* and on its first five-day voyage from La Ceiba, Honduras, in February 1900 it brought 6,000 stems of bananas into New Orleans. At first the partnership only brought a cargo to New Orleans every two to three weeks. The company survived because it was so small that it was ignored by larger rivals.

The Vaccaro Brothers developed business relationships with Italian immigrants who had moved to Honduras to farm in the 1870s. By 1905 Honduras held first place in the world's production of bananas.[12] Some shippers ordered bananas far in excess of their actual needs so that they could select only the best, leaving thousands of reject stems to rot on the beaches. Vaccaro Brothers initiated a policy of paying for whatever was ordered, whether or not loaded on the ship. This policy guaranteed the goodwill of the local farmers and assured a steady supply of fruit. Despite the growing monopoly of United Fruit in Honduras, Vaccaro Brothers was able to survive by dealing honestly with small, independent farmers.[13]

When the Vaccaros incorporated their business in 1906, it operated ten miles of railroad in Honduras, sold tropical fruit, and carried passengers by ship to Mobile, New Orleans, and Baltimore. The business continued to expand, averaging one shipment a week for a total of one million stems of bananas a year.[14] By the 1920s the company interests in Honduras included sugar mills, liquor manufactures, and industrial plants producing vegetable oil, soap, and fertilizers from the seeds of cotton, coconut, and other products grown on company lands or produced by local farmers.[15] Vaccaro Brothers reorganized in 1924 and 1926, becoming the Standard Fruit and Steamship Company.[16]

In 1964 the Vaccaro family was bought out by the international firm of Castle and Cooke, Inc., and became a wholly owned subsidiary in 1968. Standard Fruit bananas are now marketed under the Dole label.[17] (Castle and Cooke was incorporated in 1894; based in Hawaii it had interests in shipping, sugar, pineapple, nuts, seafood, and real estate.[18]) Dole and United Fruit—now Chiquita Brands International—continue to be the major importers of bananas to the United States and remain competitors to this day. In March 1973 Dole bananas moved to first place in United States sales, ahead of United Fruit for the first time with 45 percent of the market to United's 35 percent.[19]

A third major American fruit-import company, the Cuyamel Fruit Company, was founded by a Russian immigrant named Samuel Zemurray who began trading in bananas in Selma, Alabama, around 1890. He moved to Mobile and later to New Orleans where he speculated in "ripes," buying soft bananas at a low price and selling them quickly.[20] In 1902 Zemurray obtained a concession of public land in Honduras and began raising his own bananas for export.[21] Zemurray established the Cuyamel Fruit Company in 1910 and built the business to a dozen ships carrying bananas from Honduras to New Orleans and other ports. Cuyamel also built railroads, warehouses, and sugar refineries in Latin America, seriously challenging United Fruit Company.[22]

In 1929 the rivalry between Cuyamel and United Fruit was so intense that the U.S. State Department suggested a conference in Washington, D.C. The conference produced a plan for the merger of the two companies, with United Fruit buying out Cuyamel and Zemurray receiving about $20,000,000 worth of United Fruit Company shares.[23]

In addition to competition with rival companies, negotiating with foreign governments, and the ups and downs of growing and transporting bananas, the banana companies faced occasional challenges from the United States government as well. In July 1913 the Senate Finance Committee, recognizing the recent tremendous growth in banana imports, included the fruit in the proposed Underwood-Simmons Tariff. Bananas would be taxed at five cents a bunch with the hope of raising a million dollars annually.[24] The final bill would levy one-tenth of one cent per pound on bananas. The bill also included taxes of ten cents a bushel on imported apples, peaches, and other fruits. The press and lobbyists for the fruit companies claimed that the new tariff, which was supposed to be President Wilson's measure to reduce the cost of living, would actually raise the cost by taxing the "fruit of the poor man." The public responded vigorously.

The *New York Times* reported that the Atlantic Fruit Company was concerned that the tax would be destructive to smaller dealers and would result in strengthening the position of United Fruit Company, creating a monopoly. The banana tax "would bring hardship upon the poorer classes as bananas are the poor man's luxury."[25] A letter to the editor from Byron W. Holt, chairman of the Tariff Reform Committee of the Reform Club, complained that one of the campaign promises of the Democratic Party was to reduce the cost of living and that a tax on bananas would do the opposite. The writer stated that medical authorities assure us that a banana

> has a very high nutritive value. It can be obtained all year
> around—when other fruit is out of season, scarce, and high

priced, the cheap and wholesome banana can always be had. It can be cooked in a variety of ways, and the methods of cooking it are rapidly increasing. It is one of the few foods the price of which has not increased in the last ten years. The consumption is greater in the poorer districts of large cities than of any other fruit. Its sale is rapidly increasing—from 18,000,000 bunches in 1900 to 42,000,000 in 1912.[26]

Holt pointed out that as bananas could not be grown commercially in the United States, no new American industry would be established under the protection of such a tariff.

A public meeting, under the auspices of the Banana Buyers' Protective Association, was held at Cooper Union in New York City to protest the banana tax. After a band concert in the square, the meeting was addressed by Miss Julia Greenfield, age sixteen, who read a letter she had sent to President Wilson. Mrs. Julian Heath, President of the Housewives' League, and Miss Sophie Irene Loeb also spoke on the economics of the banana. Mrs. Heath claimed that the current cost of five cents for four large bananas would increase to five cents apiece under the new tariff. Miss Loeb pleaded with everyone to write to the President in protest. Harry Weinberger, Secretary of the Buyer's Association, gave an impassioned speech:

Will this tariff result in Broadway being lined with banana trees? . . . Grapes may fill the cup in Summer, apples and oranges may make indoor cheer in the Fall and Winter; the watermelon may cool and satisfy the thirst, the pineapple may keep step with the peach and the plum, and in serried ranks come forward for our delectation in the Summer time, but the only fruit that comes every day in the year, year in and year out, almost unvarying in price, within the reach of all, nutritious, healthy in its germ-proof coat, is the golden ranks of the incoming tide of bananas, 40,000,000 bunches a year, 2 to 4,000,000,000 golden satisfiers of American desires. Does Congress expect to cheapen the banana for the poor man by a tariff? They may as well add salt to the ocean, paint the lily or add a color to the rainbow, as try to benefit the consumer in this way. We say to Congress tonight "Smite us not with a tariff on bananas, while giving us honeyed words of love."[27]

Resolutions were adopted at the meeting protesting the attitude of the United States Senate in regard to the poor man's fruit.[28] The *New York Times,* in a separate article with the headline "Flying to Defend the Banana," commended the officers of the Housewives' League, and noted that the "wonderful extension of the banana trade that has marked recent years has been nothing less than a national blessing. Desperately, therefore, as the Senators are looking for sources of revenue to make up for injudicious exemptions, they should spare the banana."[29]

A delegation of prominent citizens of Jamaica traveled to New York and Washington to protest the tax. In New York they were hosted by Joseph Di Giorgio, a fruit importer, who was quoted as saying that the "imposition of this tax will be a great hardship on the poor, especially the factory workers of New England and the miners of the middle western states."[30]

Senator Williams defended the tax on bananas on the basis that they were not a basic article of food, that they were dealt in by a trust (United Fruit Company), and that the tax was so small that it would not be reflected in the price to the consumer. The *New York Times* defended the United Fruit Company "trust" stating that

the conduct of the trust has not exposed it to attack except at the hands of its trade competitors and of prejudicial politicians. The progressive cheapness of price and increase in supply, and improvement in quality in the years when the "trust" has been active show that. Never were bananas better or cheaper or more plenty than in the year when it is proposed to punish the trust by making its goods dear to its customers. Whether or not bananas are a "basic" article of food depends upon definitions and classifications. In any case, people who count their pennies do not live on basic articles of food alone. They are entitled to their little luxuries exactly because they are poor, and their luxuries are few. Consistency regarding the taxation of foods, basic or otherwise, is not a virtue of tariff makers, but the argument for free foods applies to bananas as well as to others. It is not less a food because it is toothsome and sweet.[31]

The debate was still raging at the end of August when the New York Produce Exchange began a campaign against the banana tax. As part of the campaign, Senator Root was asked to omit bananas from the tax "because they constituted the chief article of export 'from a country [Jamaica] which has evinced, in such a substantial and almost unexampled manner, her friendship for the United States.'"[32]

On September 11 the *New York Times* announced that the House "MAY ABANDON BANANA TAX." It was expected that House Democrats would insist on the rejection of the Senate amendment imposing a duty on bananas, even though the Senate expected to raise about $5,000,000 annually from bananas to offset revenue lost by shifting other articles to the free list.[33] The *Times* reported that diplomatic representatives from Costa Rica, Guatemala, Panama, and Nicaragua called at the White House to give President Wilson petitions stating that a banana tax would be ruinous to their respective countries.

John Barrett, Director General of the Pan-American Union, in mid-September sent a letter of protest to the Senate and House conferences on the tariff bill in which he portrayed the banana as a powerful civilizing influence. According to Barrett "the building up of the banana business has done more than any other individual influence, material or political, to bring about conditions of prosperity, sanitation, health, and peace in those low-lying coast lines of the Caribbean and Gulf of Mexico, which, previous to the banana era, were largely given up to wild jungles, malaria, shiftless peoples, and haunts of incipient revolutions."[34] The newspaper reported that one of the conferees suggested, after reading Barrett's letter, that the dove of peace "should hereafter carry a banana in its beak instead of the useless, if ornamental, twig of myrtle."

The banana tax was finally dropped from the Underwood-Simmons Bill and the *New York Sun* celebrated the decision with a headline that read: "THE TAX IS OFF! Bananas will be restored to the free list.—Joy Message from Washington," and the following poem by E. T. Nelson:

> Come all ye good citizens, raise
> Your loudest hosannas,
> With paeans of popular praise
> For taxless bananas.
> Food fit for the gods of Olympus,
> For doughty Dianas
> And heroes of legend: who'd skimp us
> Of blessed bananas?
>
> Meat fit for an Orient sultan,
> For dusky sultanas—
> The infant one or the adult un,
> Soul-filling bananas!
>
> Giuseppis and Abrahams eat 'em,
> And Gretchens and Hannas,
> Vox populi says you can't beat 'em,
> World-building bananas.
>
> And whether it's clay you'll be smoking
> Or fragrant Habanas,
> None thinks you are lying or joking
> If you praise bananas.
>
> They're slender and tender, nutritious,
> Most mighty of mannas;
> They're yellow and mellow, delicious—
> Praise be for bananas!
>
> You tax us for air and for water,
> For faith and bandannas;

> We go like a lamb to the slaughter—
> But halt! on bananas.

> What sound from the northernmost mountain,
> From southern savannahs?
> The East and the West are thanks shoutin'
> For untaxed bananas.[35]

World War I provided a new threat to the banana-import business, as it cut off trade between the Caribbean basin and the United States. At the outbreak of the war, the ships of the United States Merchant Marine began supplying necessary items to the Allied powers. By the time the United States declared war against Germany in April 1917, the shipping shortage was acute. United Fruit Company was required to lend thirty-seven of its largest ships to the war effort and other companies did likewise.[36] The War Trade Board suggested a complete embargo on bananas in order to free more ships for military purposes. The embargo plan was dropped but banana imports were crippled by the lack of available ships. The *Boston Globe* noted in July 1918 the arrival of 20,000 bunches of bananas from Colombia in a United Fruit steamer and the great demand for the fruit.[37] In November 1918 the headline "First Jamaican Bananas in Months" announced the imminent arrival of a banana ship to the port of Boston just as the Armistice was being signed. According to the *Boston Globe*, "scarcity of tonnage has seriously interfered with the imports of bananas at Atlantic ports since the beginning of the war."[38] Despite the scarcity, bananas continued to be available in Boston. A cartoon from July 16, 1918, with the caption "Accounting for the Mysterious Disappearance of Every One of the Banana Man's Paper Bags," showed children using the bags as gas masks while playing soldier.[39] The banana business picked up again after the war and the volume of imports continued to increase throughout the 1920s as Americans consumed more and more bananas.

In addition to wars and taxes, the fruit companies had to cope with plant disease and economic depressions. In 1927 an official from the U.S. Department of Agriculture visited United Fruit Company plantations in Tela, Honduras, and wrote a prophetic report in which he noted that:

> The economics of agriculture are rapidly changing all over the world. The increasing cost and instability of labor, the rapid decrease of virgin lands, the exhaustion of soils, and the cumulative effects of diseases and pests, all conspire to make it well worth while to plan a long way ahead for meeting the difficulties bound to arise. Plant introduction may not provide a substitute crop of the economic importance of the banana, but it may materially aid in stabilizing the banana industry and the organization around which the industry is built, through the utilization of land no longer available for bananas and which, for many reasons, can not be abandoned to the jungle.[40]

The worldwide economic depression beginning in the 1920s and extending throughout most of the 1930s, coupled with banana plant disease epidemics, hit the new international fruit companies hard. Banana prices dropped sharply in 1930 with demand for bananas falling as well. By 1932 the price of United Fruit company stock had dropped from more than $100.00 to $10.25 a share.[41] Samuel Zemurray's shares were now worth only $2,000,000 and he was furious. He obtained proxies from other large shareholders and went to Boston to seize control of the company. The Board of Directors appointed Zemurray managing director with dictatorial powers. He proceeded to fire surplus workers and cut the price the company paid for bananas it bought from independent growers. Within a month, the price of United Fruit stock more than doubled and the company was back in running order.[42]

Zemurray also brought changes to the way United Fruit Company did business in Central America. "Well aware of the hatred of Central Americans not lucky enough to share its prosperity, he tempered the irresponsible tactics that had served well enough in the freebooting days of dollar diplomacy."[43] Schools were built and staffed for workers' children and company hospitals were opened to all. In 1944 an agricultural school was opened in Honduras to train Central American farmers. In the new plantations on the Pacific coast, the company provided housing for workers that included kitchens and flush toilets. Minimum wages remained at less than a dollar a day although this was more than other local workers earned. Despite these reforms, postwar Central American governments began insisting on labor codes that required social security payments, hospitalization at company expense, and overtime pay.[44]

World War II almost brought the banana importing business to a complete halt. At the beginning of the war, the British government declared the banana a luxury, and in 1940 the sale of Jamaican bananas to the United Kingdom was halted. Deprived of its major market, Jamaica's production fell to the level needed for local consumption only.[45] The entire British-flag fleet of United Fruit Company was chartered to the British government.[46]

The United States government felt the same way about bananas, but saw a need to support the commerce of the small exporting nations in the Caribbean as long as possible. United Fruit chartered and sold some of its ships to the United States during 1941. All remaining ships were taken over by the United States government in 1942 for the duration of the war.[47] German submarine activity, the requisitioning of ships by the U.S. Navy, and the absorption of labor by the military, reduced banana imports from an average of 55 million stems per year during the 1930s to a low of 24 million in 1943.

When banana freighters were diverted for military purposes, the fruit was left to rot in the fields. A black market for bananas developed in the southern ports with high profits to the middlemen.[48] The shipping business was slow to recover from the war, being dependent upon those ships that had survived the war. Many of them were old and undermaintained.[49] *Time* magazine announced in March 1946 that banana trains were rolling again in Central America and that 100,000,000 bananas had arrived in the United States the previous week.[50] When price ceilings were lifted, bananas sold at a high price for some time having "something of the attraction of a novelty."[51] When the war ended, imports rose once again to 54 million stems in 1946.[52]

During the first half of the twentieth century, the expanding market for bananas was supplied by a steady extension of production, turning millions of acres of jungle into banana plantations, rather than by increases in yield per acre of land or per banana plant until disease forced the companies to switch to new varieties in the 1950s. Growing wild in the jungle or in small clumps in dooryards, banana plants had not been particularly susceptible to disease. Now bananas were grown by the thousands on large plantations: monoculture invited disaster.

As long as vast expanses of virgin jungle remained in Central America, when disease appeared the fruit companies could abandon their plantations and move on. By 1926 nearly 100,000 acres of jungle turned plantation had been abandoned throughout Central America.[53] The disease problem in Panama became critical once 20 percent of the banana land had been left behind.[54] As suitable land became scarce and more expensive, the companies turned to chemical herbicides and pesticides to try to control plant diseases and insect pests. Philippe Bourgois argues that United Fruit's managers actually dragged their feet in research against banana diseases as a way to maintain control of the business. The high costs of pesticides and spraying made it prohibitively expensive for other companies to compete.[55]

Sigatoka, or *Cercospora musae zimm,* is a fungus spread by wind-blown spores that attack the leaves of the banana plant and cause the fruit to ripen prematurely.[56] Healthy-looking bananas infected with sigatoka ripened aboard ship in mid-ocean and rotted before they reached port. The disease was first observed in Java in 1903, and by 1922 it had crippled banana production in Australia and New Zealand, southern China, Thailand, and Malaysia, and had spread westward to India, the Guinea coast of Africa, and the Canary Islands. Sigatoka arrived in the Americas in the late 1920s or early 1930s. By 1935 it threatened to wipe out the entire Standard

Fruit crop in Honduras.[57] In 1937 all the major banana-growing countries except Ecuador and Peru were affected, but by 1950 it had spread to these countries as well.[58] The companies considered rotating sugar with bananas and also experimented with growing cacao, cotton, rice, pineapple, and coconuts on worn-out or previously abandoned banana land.[59]

United Fruit Company began a large-scale, fixed-pipe, copper-sulfate spraying program in 1935.[60] A standard fungicide called Bordeaux mixture, made up of copper sulfate, hydrated lime, and water, was sprayed weekly on banana plants to treat Sigatoka.[61] It was effective but the cost of spraying was exorbitant.[62] Bordeaux mixture turned everything whitish-blue—the plants, the ground, and the men themselves—and lasted for days. Some growers tried dusting the plants with powdered lime from airplanes. Plane dusting proved to be less effective than liquid spray, and was gradually discontinued.[63] In the 1940s, diesel-powered giant water towers replaced irrigation ditches on the banana plantations. They could spray up to two inches of water a day over the plants during the dry season and were also used to spray Bordeaux mixture.[64] In some places, plantations were interlaced with pipes carrying the fungicide.

Spraying meant extra processing and handling when harvesting bananas because Bordeaux mixture "could eat the bottom out of a ship if it ever became mixed with salt water during the sea trip."[65] Before shipping, each bunch of fruit first had to be dipped into a cleaning solution of mild muriatic acid to remove the Bordeaux mixture and then dipped into a tank of water to remove the cleanser.[66] A side effect of this process was to eliminate any tarantulas, snakes, and other creatures that might be clinging to the bananas.

In the late 1950s, based on research in Guadaloupe, an oil-based spray for sigatoka control was developed.[67] Companies also experimented with aerial spraying of banana plantations with DDT and carbaryl to prevent insect damage. Sprayed plantations began to suffer widespread and increasingly severe outbreaks of defoliation. Evidence that plantations that were never sprayed did not suffer the heavy defoliations put a halt to wholesale spraying with insecticides in the early 1970s.[68]

A second major plant disease attacked banana plants in Panama in 1903. It was a fusarial wilt, known as Panama disease or *mal de Panama,* that attacked the roots of the plant, cutting off the water supply and choking the plant to death.[69] Thousands of acres of banana plantations had to be abandoned, and by 1910 the disease had spread to Nicaragua, Guatemala, and Costa Rica, reaching Honduras in 1926. Some growers continued to struggle against it; others moved their operations to virgin land.[70] In 1935 the Honduran town of Puerto Castilla was abandoned, along with 125 kilometers of railway that served the region.[71] By the 1940s production of bananas was almost paralyzed by the disease, and companies moved their plantations to the Pacific coast.[72]

In the 1950s disease and strong winds decimated the Gros Michel banana plants that had been the mainstay of the imported banana trade for the past fifty years. Fruit companies began to experiment with new disease-resistant varieties of bananas that were also less prone to be blown down in wind storms, and their fortunes began to recover. During the early 1950s in the Caribbean islands, and in the late 1950s in Honduras, plantations were converted to wilt-resistant varieties of the Cavendish subgroup of banana plants.[73] Cavendish varieties were planted throughout Central America, Panama, and South America by 1970.[74]

The yield per unit of land more than doubled with the new varieties. Cavendish plants yielded between 2,500 and 3,000 eighteen-kilogram boxes per hectare compared with 1,000–1,200 boxes for Gros Michel. Instead of ever-expanding banana plantations, the new high-yield plants resulted in the release of large areas of land formerly planted with Gros Michel now held in reserve for other crops and livestock.[75]

In the 1960s large tracts of suitable virgin land were no longer available in Central America, and growers there were forced to replant their fields with the new disease-resistant bananas. By 1970 the conversion was completed. In South America, the conversion began in the late 1960s and was completed by 1975 with the exception of an area of Gros Michel plantations in northern Ecuador grown mostly for home consumption.[76] Today the Cavendish is the standard large yellow banana found in grocery stores and supermarkets. The changeover and increased yield of the new plants resulted in the first widespread oversupply of bananas in 1971, with accompanying depressed prices. A second glut of fruit occurred in 1982 with heavy losses for the banana-importing companies.[77]

Banana growers in Honduras faced yet another crisis in 1972 when a fungus called black sigatoka began attacking the leaves of the Cavendish banana plants. The fungus was airborne and destroyed the leaves of the plant which are critical for shielding the young fruit.[78] Black sigatoka was much more virulent than its predecessor and reduced the yield from each plant by 30 to 50 percent.[79] By the early 1980s, the fungus had spread from Honduras to the rest of Central America, and by 1987 it had reached Ecuador. In that year, Central American banana growers spent $100 million to control the disease, in some areas nearly a third of the total growing costs.[80]

Today growers control sigatoka and the new strains of Panama disease that attack the Cavendish plants with fungicides, but scientists worry that the diseases are developing a tolerance to the latest generation of chemical weapons. Banana plantations around the world are in trouble; in West and Central Africa, banana harvests have been cut in half since the mid-1980s.[81]

The answer may be the development of a new disease-resistant banana to succeed the Cavendish. Philip Rowe, a plant breeder who has worked for United Fruit and is now working for a Honduran agricultural research foundation, has spent the past twenty years looking for a better banana. His current candidate, the Goldfinger, thrives in different parts of the world but is not yet an acceptable dessert banana. Taste panels have described the fruit as "too acidic and too starchy."[82] Rowe's current research is using a dwarf Gros Michel banana to develop Goldfinger II, hoping to produce a reasonable facsimile and substitute for the Cavendish.

In the 1960s yet another banana pest began to attack banana plants when nematodes, microscopic worms that feed on the roots of plants, began to multiply dramatically. Dow Chemical and Shell Oil came up with dibromochloropropane (DBCP) that killed the nematodes without hurting the plants. Workers mixed the chemical with water and injected it into the soil around the base of the banana plants with giant hypodermic needles. Banana yields increased by 30 percent and DBCP was widely used. Unfortunately the chemical is indicated in damaging the testicles and reducing sperm count in laboratory animals, and has been linked with fertility problems in the workers on banana plantations and in the United States. DBCP has been banned in the continental United States since 1979 but it is still used in banana-producing countries.[83]

Another insecticide, Aldicarb, was introduced to the market in 1970 to control mites and nematodes. It was also applied by spraying and could be absorbed by the edible part of the fruit. Environmental Protection Agency staff recommended that the chemical be banned for banana use in 1989 when it was found to cause symptoms ranging from headache and stomach upset to blurred vision, disorientation, and seizures, but the agency never took action. In 1991 the EPA reported that a small percentage of imported bananas had been found tainted with Aldicarb and initiated a ninety-day testing program for all banana imports although there were no reports of illness due to eating bananas. The manufacturer, Rhone-Poulenc, promptly withdrew the product from the market for use on bananas. It had been withdrawn for use on potatoes the previous year after field tests showed excessive residue levels. It remains in use on citrus, soybeans, coffee beans, sweet potatoes, sugar beets, pecans, tobacco, cotton and alfalfa seeds.[84]

Pesticides and herbicides banned in the United States but used on banana plantations in Central America began to spark concern in the United States in the 1980s when a multimillion dollar law suit was filed against several U.S. companies in American courts on behalf of thousands of Costa Rican farm workers who claimed that they had been made sterile by exposure to DVCP. The suit was settled out of court in Texas in 1992.[85]

In 1993 *World Watch* reported that after the 1991 proposal of an international boycott of Costa Rican bananas, the Costa Rican government and multinational fruit growers finally had begun to act. The search for pest-resistant varieties of banana plants continues and on many plantations spraying is done on an as-needed basis rather than on a fixed schedule. Environment-friendly bananas are being promoted by the Banana Amigo Project, sponsored by the U.S.–based Rainforest Alliance as well as Fundacíon Ambio and Tsuli Tsuli/Audubon of Costa Rica. Some American activists claim that banana growers such as Chiquita Brands International have responded by hiring banana workers for six-month contracts instead of permanently so that the workers are let go before serious health problems related to pesticide and fungicide use can be detected.[86]

Both Del Monte and Standard Fruit took a considerable share of the banana market away from United Fruit during the 1970s. The low for United Fruit was reached with losses of $47 million in 1974 and a take-over by new owners in 1976.[87] By 1983 United Fruit and Standard Fruit each claimed about one-third of the U.S. market and Del Monte and other small importers had the other third.[88] Along with a decline in market share, United Fruit drastically reduced its plantations in Central America from about 54,000 hectares in 1954 to 15,000 in 1984.[89]

United Fruit became part of the larger conglomerate named United Brands in June 1970 when it merged with AMK Corporation. AMK, originally a producer of milk-bottle caps, managed to acquire the fourth largest meatpacker in the United States, John Morrell and Company, during the 1960s. In 1969 AMK acquired a majority share of United Fruit Company. After some negotiation with the Federal Trade Commission, concerned by the antitrust implications, the new United Brands was incorporated. In 1974 the Union de Paises Exportadores de Banano (UPEB) was formed by the banana-producing countries of Costa Rica, Guatemala, Honduras, and Panama. The UPEB was later joined by Colombia, Nicaragua, and the Dominican Republic. These countries agreed to levy large banana export taxes which were strongly opposed by the transnational fruit companies. This led to a brief so-called "banana war."[90] In the next few years, United Brands experienced the worst losses in its history. In addition to taxes, hurricane Fifi hit Central America in 1974, wiping out 70 percent of the company's plantations in Honduras with losses of more than $20 million. Company chairman, Eli Black, committed suicide in February 1975.[91]

In April the Securities and Exchange Commission charged United Brands with paying a bribe of $1.25 million and agreeing to pay another $1.25 million to a Honduran official in exchange for a reduction in export taxes. Trade in United Brands stock was halted for almost a week, the president of Honduras was removed in a military coup on suspicion of participating in the bribe, and the government of Costa Rica threatened to cancel all contracts with United Brands. Finally a federal grand jury brought criminal charges against the company. In 1978 the company pleaded guilty to conspiring to pay $2.5 million to the former Honduran minister of the economy and was fined the maximum penalty of $15,000.[92]

A series of chairmen and presidents managed to keep United Brands afloat until 1984, but profits slipped and net losses steadily increased. Carl Linder took over as chairman and shifted away from large, diversified operations toward a narrower focus throughout the company, selling off soft drinks, animal feeds, and international telecommunications. The company was renamed Chiquita Brands International and headquarters were moved from New York to Cincinnati.[93]

Frozen fruit pops were added to the Chiquita product line but the company lost $10 million in 1987. The company was more successful in using the Chiquita name to sell other fresh fruit. In the late 1980s Chiquita recaptured first place in the banana market from Dole which had taken the lead from Chiquita in the early 1970s. By 1990 the company had stabilized and appeared to be "at a higher level of financial and managerial operation than it has ever been before."[94]

Standard Fruit became part of Castle and Cooke, and Del Monte was purchased by R. J. Reynolds in 1979.[95] Bananas became just one part of the corporate interest, playing an ever-smaller role in corporate sales and earnings. Castle and Cooke was purchased by David Murdock in 1985 and renamed Dole Corporation.[96] Dole sold more than a hundred kinds of fresh fruits and vegetables, packaged foods, juices, and nuts, with extensive real estate holdings in Hawaii and in California. Murdock put the food division up for sale in August 1990. He quickly pulled it off the market in December when the banana markets in Europe began to expand.[97] That year a third of Dole's sales and as much as 40 percent of the food division's operating profits of $205 million came from bananas while pineapple made up less than 10 percent.[98]

In 1990 Chiquita Brands International controlled about 33 percent of the global market with Dole close behind with an estimated 22 percent share.[99] The banana wars continued. In the mid-1990s, the United States, on behalf Chiquita Brands International and Dole Food Company, challenged the European Union through the World Trade Organization to block the Caribbean's continued access to the European market for its banana exports. Leaders of former colonial nations in Africa, the Caribbean, and the Pacific, whose economies were heavily dependent on banana exports to Europe, maintained that any changes to the EU preferences would damage their banana-dependent economies, and that they could not compete against Latin American fruit in an open market.

Former senator Robert Dole lobbied the Clinton administration with great success, and the World Trade Organization ruled in support of a United States complaint that European Union preferences to its former colonies were discriminatory. Caribbean governments then warned that denying them access would cause economic, political, and social destabilization throughout the entire region since, in some countries, banana exports accounted for some 70 percent of total export earnings.[100]

In November 1998 the United States threatened to slap 100 percent tariffs on a list of European products unless the EU changed its preferential treatment for Caribbean, African, and Pacific producers.[101] Europeans objected that "not a single American banana is involved, and not a single American job is at stake. To think that one interest group can create such a row. . . . This is a very extreme example when you have one narrow pressure group pushing the United States toward a trade war with Europe."[102] In April 1999 the World Trade Organization determined that American commercial interests had suffered losses of $191.4 million in each of the years the European Union regime had existed, for a total of more than $1 billion in harm.[103] The European Union refused to bring its system into World Trade Organization conformity and the United States retaliated by slapping sanctions on European businesses not directly involved in the dispute. And the fight continues to this very day.

In May 1998 the *Cincinnati Enquirer* published a series of articles by two investigative reporters, Mike Gallagher and Cameron McWhirter, exposing a range of questionable business practices by the hometown company, Chiquita Brands International, Inc. These articles led to suits by stockholders against Chiquita charging that the company violated its duties by engaging in illegal acts, gross mismanagement, and abuse of corporate control in Colombia and Honduras.[104] Chiquita Brands in turn sued the newspaper on the grounds that the reporters had used illegally obtained voice-mail tapes. The *Enquirer* fired the reporters, apologized to Chiquita Brands, and repudiated the series, but there was never any challenge to the facts that had been reported.

Hurricane Mitch devastated Honduras, Nicaragua, and Guatemala in November 1998, destroying 90 percent of the entire banana industry in Honduras. At the time Honduras was the fourth largest banana producer, exporting six billion bananas a year. The storm threw thousands of people out of work on banana plantations and was expected to wipe out $255 million in annual banana exports over the next two years before the industry might begin to recover.[105] Chiquita laid off all of its 7,400 workers while mapping out a reconstruction plan. The company promised to keep schools open, to continue to provide workers and their families with medical insurance, housing, and utility service, and to provide employees with two months of financial assistance. After that employees would be eligible for interest-free loans.[106] Dole began shipping food, medicine, and other supplies to Puerto Cortes in Honduras. The hardest hit were small farmers who sold their own crops to the major companies and had no resources or support to rebuild.

In 1990 the world ate an estimated 16 billion pounds or about 42 billion bananas. In a little over one hundred years, the banana business developed from ship captains with occasional cargoes of bananas enjoyed as luxury items in North American port cities to multinational corporations with worldwide markets dealing in billions of pounds and billions of dollars worth of fruit, enjoying the protection of the federal government. Would Captain Baker and Charles Frank be amazed or would they feel vindicated?

3

TRANSPORTING
Bananas

BANANAS DID NOT FIGURE AS A plantation or export crop during the colonial era in the Caribbean and Central America, mainly because of the difficulty of transporting them to distant markets. Although bananas found a ready market in schooner days, they remained a luxury item until the introduction of steamships, the extension of the railroad throughout the United States, and the availability of refrigeration. These innovations made it possible to cut the time in transit and to keep the fruit at a constant temperature to slow the ripening process.

Bananas entered North American markets and became important in the culture and diet of the United States partly as a result of the transportation revolution that began in the latter part of the nineteenth century. Beginning with the railroads and quickly followed by steamships and then trucking, and eventually an interstate road system, Americans spread out across an immense continent while remaining connected with the cities and ports on the East and West coasts. Mail-order catalogs and a growing wholesale and retail network meant that the goods enjoyed in one area of the country were soon available to all.

The first official banana importation was recorded in the United

States in 1804 when the schooner *Reynard* brought thirty stalks of red bananas to New York from Cuba.[1] Banana importing was a risky business for sailing vessels. Contrary winds or calm seas might extend the length of the voyage, and the fruit would ripen and rot before reaching East Coast ports such as Philadelphia, New York, and Boston. Ship captains and crews sometimes brought a few stalks on board for themselves and if any of the remaining bananas reached port in salable condition, they might make a nice profit. Usually they did not.

Sporadic attempts at banana importing during the mid-nineteenth century by American entrepreneurs brought small quantities of produce from independent growers in the Caribbean and Central America. In 1830 Capt. John Pearsall included fifteen hundred stalks of bananas in the cargo of the *Harriet Smith*.[2] Pearsall is credited with being the first to risk bringing a full cargo of bananas to the port of New York. It is possible that these are the bananas that James Fenimore Cooper referred to when he reported that "bannanas" could be found in the New York market.[3]

It was not until 1843 that official port records first listed bananas. That year a commission merchant imported three hundred bunches of Cuban reds and sold the lot at twenty-five cents a finger, over two dollars apiece in today's money.[4] Some years later, the merchant was forced to declare bankruptcy when a shipment of three thousand bunches reached port too ripe to sell.[5]

By 1850 cargoes of Cuban bananas were being delivered to New York, Philadelphia, and Baltimore.[6] Pushcart peddlers, waiting at the dock, bought a few bunches at a time first come, first served. But other than these occasional small shipments to East Coast ports, bananas were virtually unknown in the United States before the Civil War.

As the banana trade increased, fruit import companies were formed to purchase bananas by the shipload. In the Caribbean islands, company representatives sent messengers to interior farms telling growers that a ship would reach a certain coastal site on a given day prepared to select and purchase bananas. The bananas were transported to the coast from the interior by river, canals, rail-road, "or, when these are not available, on the heads of women" and were left to accumulate until the steamer arrived.[7]

At first there were few harbors in the banana-growing areas. Ships anchored offshore and the fruit was loaded onto small boats by men, women, and children who waded out to them carrying each stem of bananas overhead to avoid the salt water. The full boats were poled beyond the breakers to the anchored ship and the bananas were taken up by rope nets.[8] Because of the perishability of the fruit, the growers were always in a hurry to sell and the American merchants were able to keep prices low. The merchants in turn faced risks of heavy losses during the voyage to North American ports and also fierce competition with each other.

United Fruit was the first to achieve a constant, year-round flow of bananas to North American cities.[9] The company created a re-frigerated distribution network comparable to that of meatpackers and produced a truly national market. A 1904 United Fruit Com-pany booklet noted that "the secret of success lies in having the fruit properly grown, cut at the right time, handled without bruising, bringing it into the Northern markets before the green fruit begins to color, and then distributing it immediately to consumers with every item of expense kept at the lowest point"[10]—more easily said than done.

United Fruit was so successful that it was accused of monopolis-tic practices by the American Banana Company, and an investiga-tion was launched by the Committee on Interstate Commerce of the United States Senate in 1908. In its defense, United Fruit noted that

the only advantage which one person engaged in the trade can have over another is the extent and perfection of its equipment and organization. These . . . are substantial advantages, and, when in addition one person or corporation can own its own plantations and adopt improved methods of planting, cultiva-tion, and handling, this gives such person a very great advan-tage as he is thus enabled to produce fruit of superior quality at little additional cost.[11]

"Conveying Fruit from Cars to Steamship, *Story of the Banana,* United
Fruit, Boston, 1921, 36.

The report concluded that "the operations of the United Fruit
Company have so increased the market for bananas at all points,
and have so organized the trade, that any one introducing bananas
at the seaboard finds a large independent market not at all bound
to the United Fruit Company, and which is open to anyone who can
deliver proper bananas at competitive prices."[12] The committee ac-
cepted this argument, and serious charges of monopolistic practices were not again faced until the 1950s.

In the beginning, banana ships were unloaded by workers who
carried each of the 100- to 150-pound stems of fruit out of the
holds. A cargo of 35,000 stems took 400 laborers seven to eight
hours to move from the ship to waiting railroad freight cars.[13] The
men stood in a long line extending from the ship's interior to the
waiting freight cars on the dock, and each stalk would be handed
from man to man until it reached the appropriate car.[14]

In 1903 the first unloading machine was introduced in Mobile and then in New Orleans. A circular chain dipped canvas buckets into the hold where longshoremen placed one stem in each bucket to be lifted to the deck. The buckets could move 2,500 stems an hour, far faster than any number of men could carry the fruit, with big savings for the fruit companies.[15] An electrically driven conveyor system was put into operation in Galveston, Texas, and was described as follows:

> Ranged along the fruit wharf are a number of odd looking pyramidal houses each with a sort of an elephant trunk protruding from their sides. These are the electrically operated fruit conveyors. As soon as the ship is laid alongside, the trunk swings out and drops a long conveyor belt down through the hatches into the hold. Then the wheels begin to turn and the canvas pockets travel in an endless succession from the hold to the wharf. Down in the hold the men lay the bunches of bananas onto the conveyor, placing a single bunch in each pocket as it presents itself. As the bunches reach the wharf end they are taken by men who hurry them off to the various railroad cars on nearby tracks. The wharf appears then to be swarming with moving bunches of bananas set on two legs.[16]

One of the problems with this new machine was that it was too fast for human workers and could only be run for forty minutes every hour. By 1920 the conveyors were extended to a dockside monorail trolley system to reach the waiting freight cars, and the fruit was transferred almost without human handling. The new system saved three hours per ship and displaced at least 400 jobs at a cost savings of 2.5 cents a stalk. It was estimated that the total "annual saving will not greatly miss the million mark."[17]

In winter weather, the fruit was warmed up several degrees in the ship's hold before unloading, and the unloading machines were sheltered with canvas canopies to protect the fruit from the cold.[18] On the dock bananas were loaded onto railroad cars and trucks, each stem counted by automatic tally machines. Fruit that showed evidence of damage or was too ripe to ship further was sold locally at reduced prices.

Most fruit companies chartered or leased from Norwegian or British owners ships built in Europe specifically for the banana trade.[19] In 1900 United Fruit out of Boston had thirty-six steamers, the "Southern Fleet," that carried fruit to New Orleans and Mobile as well as to more northern East Coast ports.[20] Another twenty worked out of the ports of Boston, New York, Philadelphia, and Baltimore.[21] By 1915 United Fruit was operating a fleet of ninety-five ships.[22] The ships had 5,000-ton capacities, carrying 40,000 bunches of bananas each trip.[23]

The S.S. *Venus,* the first refrigerated produce boat, was launched in 1903. In that year, United Fruit Company imported from its Caribbean holdings 1¼ billion pounds of bananas.[24] By 1905 banana imports reached 33 million bunches, over 3½ billion pieces of fruit, an average of forty bananas a year for each person in the United States.[25]

By 1920 United Fruit had become one of the largest enterprises in the United States, with a vertically integrated network of plantations, refrigerated steamships, and railroad cars to produce, transport, distribute, and market bananas.[26] In addition to bananas, the Great White Fleet carried passengers, mail, and other merchandise between Caribbean and North American ports. A second fleet, painted gray, operated between the Caribbean and Europe.[27] Banana ships carried freight and mail on return trips to the Caribbean using otherwise empty cargo space. Many of these ships were equipped with comfortable passenger cabins, and the service rivaled that of the transcontinental railroads. In 1902 over 5,500 people chose to travel on the banana boats.[28] A 1904 publication described United Fruit's steamship passenger service as follows:

> The "Admiral" steamships operated by this company are American built twin-screw vessels, and are especially adapted to tropical travel. They have commodious promenade decks, cool and airy, well-ventilated staterooms situated on the main and hurri-

United Fruit Company's Fleet, J. M. Hill, *A Short History of the Banana and a Few Recipes for Its Use* (Boston, United Fruit, 1904), 32.

cane decks amidships, thus insuring a minimum of sea motion. The dining saloon is located on the main deck well forward of the engine room, and removed from all disagreeable odors incident. Bathrooms are supplied with fresh or sea water and are at the disposal of passengers at all times.

The table is made an especial feature of these boats, and is supplied with every delicacy the northern and tropical markets afford.

The ships are furnished throughout with a perfect system of electric lighting and steam heating.

The stewards and waiters are unremitting in their duties

and everything is done for the comfort and convenience of the passengers.[29]

The company also built hotels in Jamaica and other popular destinations. United Fruit promoted tourism and established a separate passenger department featuring special tropical cruises. They published travel guides such as "A Happy Month in Jamaica" (c. 1915) in which potential tourists or armchair travelers could look at lots of black-and-white photographs and read descriptions of what to see and where to stay. Concerns about foreign travel were soothed with assurances that disembarkation "at the wharf of a modern American hotel [is] conducted in the best American method; on landing, greedy native porters do not snatch our baggage and quarrel about the fees."[30] The fare from Boston, New York, or Philadelphia to Port Antonio (including meals and berth in stateroom) was $40 one way and $75 round trip. Fares were $35 and $70 from Baltimore.

Businessmen in 1918 were assured that the accommodations and cuisine on the ships of the Great White Fleet were on a par with those of their favorite club or hotel and that they would be "free to enjoy the salt air, sunshine and relaxation of a sea voyage—without the petty annoyance caused by inferior quarters or service."[31] A travelogue for a "Great White Fleet Caribbean Cruise" published in 1922 gave a highly romantic account of the various ports of call including Cuba, Jamaica, Panama, Costa Rica, Colombia, and Guatemala. Potential customers were assured that

the steamships are all especially designed for cruising in the Caribbean Sea and while some are a little larger than others, the same high standard of service is aimed at for all. They are the most expensively constructed vessels of their kind in the world. All cruise staterooms are outside and are first class only. Not how large, but how fine, best expresses the thought dominating the construction of the ships of the Great White Fleet; a steamship service designed to meet the most exacting requirements of the traveler.[32]

In 1928, at the height of its success, the Great White Fleet numbered a hundred vessels and carried 70,000 passengers, 250,000 bags of mail, and 56 million stems of bananas.[33]

Standard Fruit entered the tourist business in 1926, with service from New Orleans to the Caribbean.[34] In the early 1930s Standard Fruit moved into direct competition with United Fruit for banana trade in Central America, and for the tourist trade in North America. Standard offered twelve-day cruise service to Nassau and Kingston from New York as well as package tours to Cuba, Mexico, and Honduras.[35]

At the height of the Depression, United Fruit Company advertised its "30th Successful Season" of guest cruises to the West Indies and Caribbean:

> Thirty years . . . and now the "Guest Cruises" of 1933! As in 1903, here is the truly intimate way to enjoy the tropics . . . with six new, magnificent liners now leading a finer Great White Fleet! Every spotless vessel in the service was built for the tropics, its men trained in the tropics, its free-handed, personalized service perfected for tropical cruising . . . in the favorite informal manner. With outdoor swimming pools and other modern shipboard facilities, with the superb cooking that helped make these ships famous, and with adept staffs afloat and ashore whose pleasure it is to make you comfortable, these are the cruises preferred by those who KNOW the tropics . . . and no wonder![36]

The cost began at $125 from New York or $97.50 from New Orleans, and it was possible to travel from New York to California for $200, $300 for the round trip.

Tourism dropped during the Depression years of the 1930s and came to a halt during World War II. At the end of the war, United Fruit moved the basis of its operations from the Caribbean to the Pacific coast of Central America. It was expected that the company "would continue to accommodate passengers in spite of the Great

White Fleet's unofficial motto: 'Every banana a guest, every passenger a pest.' "[37] An illustration in a 1954 United Fruit Company
magazine shows passengers, mostly women, in bathing suits relax-
ing in deck chairs while being served bananas from a tray.[38]

Beginning in the 1880s, technical advances in steamships, railroads, and refrigeration made it possible to transport perishable
tropical merchandise such as bananas to all parts of North America.[39] The nationwide network of railroads that developed after the
Civil War not only enabled farmers to transport their crops to
seaboard cities and foreign markets, but also meant that foreign
products such as bananas could be distributed throughout the
country. In 1885 a weekly cookery journal noted with some exag-
geration that

> one of the best evidences that the American people of this gen-
> eration live better than their fathers did is found in the steady
> and rapid growth of the trade in tropical fruits. It is not many
> years since the great majority of people scarcely knew what a ba-
> nana was, and considered oranges and lemons as luxuries to be
> afforded only in sickness or on great occasions. Now, not only
> these, but other tropical fruits, are brought and eaten almost as
> generally and freely as apples, and the consumption of melons,
> peaches, pears, plums and berries, is on the same universal and
> extensive scale. This is a change which tends to gratify the taste,
> and to promote health, which is the foundation of human hap-
> piness, and is of advantage to everybody.[40]

A decade later a cookbook author extolled the railroads that were
bringing

> early fruits from the far South and late fruits from the far
> North, so that at the centres of population the several fruit sea-
> sons are delightfully prolonged. Nor are we restricted to our
> own country's production. Such are the facilities for rapid and

safe communication from distant points that the world lays her tribute of fruits, sweet and sound, at the door of the enlightened nations.[41]

In order to sell billions of pounds of bananas to the people of the United States, the fruit companies had to establish wholesale and retail networks to move the fruit to the consumer. Profits lay in efficient distribution and sales, as well as the total volume of fruit sold.[42] Bananas have to be harvested fully developed but green enough to stand a journey of anywhere from five to eighteen days before ripening to a yellow color with brownish flecks. At first the stems were hung in tiers, in stalls, or boxes built of slats, in the between-decks of steamers where they would get the most air cir-

Stowing the bunches, J. Mace Andress and Julia E. Dickson, *Radio Bound for Banana Land,* Education Department (Boston: United Fruit, 1932), 15.

culation.[43] Later steamships with refrigerated holds kept the cargo at a constant temperature of 57°F to prevent the fruit from ripening too quickly on the voyage.[44]

New Orleans was a logical port for the banana trade. It was the closest major American port to the Caribbean and it was the hub of an expanding railroad network that ran up the Mississippi River. A large market developed in the growing Midwestern cities and towns at the turn of the century. By 1905 New Orleans was the largest fruit-importing port in the world, distributing more than nine million stems of bananas by rail to the cities in the interior of the United States.[45]

The first ventilated railroad car for transporting fruit resembled a large cage with iron bars, on the theory that the more ventilation the better the fruit would "carry." When the Armour meatpacking company designed an improved slat-sided freight car it was quickly adopted for banana transport.[46] In 1910 over 60,000 freight cars, each containing 500 bunches were dispatched throughout the United States.[47] The Fruit Dispatch Company claimed that it was the first to successfully ship bananas under ice. This experiment was undertaken in response to the refusal of storekeepers in certain sections of the country to handle bananas during the summer months because of the risk in transit and their inability to sell the fruit without significant losses. By 1920 all companies had adopted the use of ice to cool banana freight cars, and in the warm months of 1923 the southern division of the Fruit Dispatch Company alone used 29,731 tons of ice.[48]

One of the beauties of the banana business was that the freight moved inland from the port cities in the opposite direction to the bulk of other railroad traffic, making economical use of freight cars. Banana trains consisted of from twenty to one hundred cars and maintained fast schedules.[49] In 1927 it took 55 hours for bananas to travel from New Orleans to Chicago, 88 hours to Minneapolis, 184 hours to Seattle, and 208 hours (nearly nine days) to Vancouver.[50] From the ports of New York and Philadelphia, the fruit was shipped to Cleveland, Detroit, and Toronto in about 36 hours.

The main line from New Orleans ran along the Mississippi River to Fulton, Kentucky, where five railroad lines met. Fulton became known as the Banana Capital of the World (see Chapter 7). At first the Fruit Dispatch Company and other import companies sent "messengers," often Italian, with each train to look after the perishable freight. Their job was to inspect cars and test the temperature of sample fruit by sticking thermometers into random bananas. The cars could be either iced, heated, or the ventilation slats adjusted according to the weather and the condition of the fruit. By 1923 resident messengers were stationed at strategic divisional and junction points along the route such as Fulton, Dubuque, Iowa, and Mounds, Illinois.[51] The boxcars were then dispatched north, east, and west. Messengers and the men stationed at strategic checkpoints also reported to each other on existing and predicted weather conditions along the route.

Ice companies in New Orleans and at stops along the way supplied large blocks of ice that were inserted into compartments at either end of the railroad cars during hot weather. The ice racks were

Icing cars of bananas at New Orleans, *Story of the Banana*, Education Department (Boston: United Fruit, 1921), 44.

elevated to prevent over-refrigeration of the bottom layers of fruit.[52] Standard Fruit managed to buy up most of the ice plants in New Orleans after 1915, and its President Joseph Vaccaro became known as the "Ice King."[53]

In cold months the boxcars were papered at the bulkheads and doorways, and straw protected the fruit. As an added precaution, kerosene, oil, or charcoal heaters could be used to warm the cars.[54] In the northern ports, banana boxcars were heated before they were loaded and, in particularly cold weather, again after they were loaded before being sent on their way. There were several large heating plants, one located at Rouses Point, New York, for shipments to Canada, one at Mounds, Illinois, and another at Dubuque, Iowa. The facilities in Illinois and Iowa were for shipments from southern ports heading north and northwest. The plant at Mounds was the largest and could handle seventy-two freight cars at one time.[55] A large cooling and heating plant in Springfield, Missouri, built by the St. Louis and San Francisco Railroad Company, consisted of four tracks inside a shed. Each track could hold ten freight cars. Large air ducts crossed the roof of the shed, and canvas tubes carried warm or cool air into one end of the freight car and took it out at the other after passing through the fruit.[56]

Another peril of the shipping business was constantly changing regulations concerning disease in southern U.S. cities. In a 1905 yellow fever epidemic that swept the ports of the Gulf Coast, 452 lives were lost in New Orleans and perhaps as many more in other areas of the South. Quarantines requiring a fifteen-day fumigation period were imposed against ships from the tropics, often without notice. This was particularly hard for perishable produce such as bananas that when spoiled were dumped into the Mississippi River.[57]

The public blamed epidemics on the fruit industry with its ties to the tropics, and specifically the Italians working on the ships and on the railroads in the United States.[58] In the 1905 epidemic, the port of New Orleans refused to allow bananas to enter or leave the city. Montgomery, Alabama, prohibited the entry of all bananas until frost. The town of Mounds, Illinois, asked the state board of health to prohibit the passage of banana trains through the state, fearing that the messengers would infect them with yellow fever.[59] Once the epidemic was over, the banana trade quickly returned to its normal level.

In the 1920s and 1930s the banana market in the western United States was supplied by ships that crossed through the Panama Canal and sailed to West Coast ports. This cut the time of transportation significantly from the six- to nine-day train trip to the West Coast from the port of New Orleans. Standard Fruit plantations in Mexico served the southwest by railway until labor unrest forced the company out of the country.[60] Direct shipments to Canadian ports on the Atlantic and Pacific coasts in the 1930s also cut some of the banana traffic in the United States. In the summer months, bananas could be found even beyond the Arctic Circle.[61]

After World War I, Americans began to demand better roads for the ever-increasing number of automobiles and trucks. Trucks had proven their worth during the war in Europe but needed an extensive system of paved roads. In 1921 Congress passed the Federal Highway Act, providing federal aid for state roads. In 1923 the Bureau of Public Roads began to plan a national highway system. By 1930 efficient truck services to small towns at first supplemented but ultimately supplanted the railway system in the United States. Trucking began to affect a wide range of American life from manufacturing plant location to eating habits, and more transport firms appeared to deliver goods to the expanding consumer-oriented society motivated by advertising.[62] Towns heretofore unserved by railroads could be efficiently served by truck routes, and bananas found their way into shops and stores even in small villages throughout the nation.

The road system grew slowly during the 1920s and then construction came to a halt with the Depression until the Works Progress Administration was authorized in 1935. Between 1935 and 1943 the WPA was responsible for building over 650,000 miles of highways, streets, and roads.[63] With the expansion of the road system, trucks began to compete with the railroads in regional and national markets. They changed distribution patterns, upset established markets, and opened up new venues. It is estimated that during this period trucking brought the final 10 percent of the population, once isolated from major railroad arteries, into contact with the national economy.[64]

Refrigerated trucks began to compete with railroads for the banana business in the 1940s. At first, trucks were insulated with grass and sawdust and cooled by barrels of water and ice. The technology of refrigeration improved with the adoption of dry ice and later mechanical devices. One entrepreneur, Everett Lawrence, built up a fleet of thirty-four trucks to haul bananas to Midwestern markets previously supplied by rail. Trucking the fruit cost about half as much as by rail in the early 1950s, and the railroad banana freight business began to decline.[65]

The Highway Act of 1956 dealt a severe blow to the railroads. The law resulted in the construction of a 41,000-mile interstate highway system intended to assist commerce. This network connected all the major cities and important industrial areas in the country. It was fed by county, state, and national highways, and provided a much more complete system than that of the railroads.

Another advantage in truck transportation was that truckers charged flat rates with no extra charges for loading and unloading or for refrigerating the cargo. Railroads offered these services and arranged for carting small shipments to retail stores but charged extra for these services. Not all trucking was cheaper than rail transport, but the savings in time and in the reduction in handling perishable goods often offset higher rates.[66]

By the 1970s fruit companies had largely abandoned freight trains in favor of refrigerated tractor-trailer trucks to transport bananas to every hamlet and corner store in America.

4

SELLING

Bananas

THE INDUSTRIAL REVOLUTION OF THE eighteenth and nineteenth centuries and the increasing sophistication of capitalism focused the mass market and the belief that demand would expand to meet supply. The idea of pricing bananas low enough so that everyone could buy them and still make a profit for the producing company preceded Henry Ford's Model T. The major banana-importing companies set up marketing divisions and educational programs to convince Americans that the banana was an essential item to be eaten every day. Not only did bananas taste good; they were good for you. If consumers could be convinced to include bananas in every meal as well as in between-meal snacks, the market would be limited only by the quantity of fruit that could be grown.

The small import companies of the nineteenth century proved that there was a market for bananas in the United States if the fruit were offered at prices that could compete with local apples, peaches, pears, and oranges.[1] Bananas lost their elite luxury status and disappeared from the dinner tables of the wealthy, transformed through low price, year-round availability, and abundance into comfort food for children and the elderly. Today bananas seldom appear on elegant menus because they are considered plebeian. The fruit that began its career in the Americas as a food for slaves became in the nineteenth century an exotic luxury for wealthy and well-traveled North Americans, then entered the twentieth century as the poor man's food. A new cycle began when the banana was incorporated into the diets of the middle and upper classes where it was deemed important for good health.

What turned an exotic, foreign, and costly fruit into the daily fare of even the poorest American? Did Americans begin to eat bananas simply because they liked them, or were there other reasons for the enormous popularity of the imported fruit? Low cost was certainly a factor. Increasing availability throughout the year was another. Ease of preparation was a third. In addition, a new food has to be thought of as tasting good before a person will try it. Advertising and other promotional activities kept the banana fresh in the minds, if not in the mouths, of most residents of the United States.

In the tropics banana plantations can be managed so that fruit is continually coming to harvest year-round. This is an advantage that is harder to grasp today when we expect to find a wide variety of fruit at the grocery store; apples, kiwi fruit, grapes, even strawberries and raspberries are available to us year-round albeit at a higher price. Another advantage that bananas had was that they were always the same despite the season. Americans do not like surprises with their food and value consistency, as Howard Johnson and later McDonald's and other chain restaurants have made abundantly clear.

Until the mid-nineteenth century, fresh fruits and vegetables were eaten when they were harvested, and only fruit preserved by drying or canning was available during the winter and spring months. In the 1890s steamship and railroad networks were able to bring fresh semitropical and tropical fruit and vegetables to households throughout the United States, enriching American diets with much needed vitamins and varying the menu. Bananas were incorporated in the diet in place of other seasonal fruit, interchangeable, cheaper, and consistently available.

At first, bananas were sold in East Coast ports from the ships they arrived on to anyone who would carry them away. The fruit was sold by the stem, each with as many as a hundred fingers or twenty hands. Wholesale buyers were able to select their own fruit as they only bought a few stems at a time.

As the demand for bananas grew stronger, the fruit began to be sold by the "steamer run," as it came out of the ship.[2] An 1894 article in *Harper's Weekly* noted that it took a crowd of stevedores, twenty wagons, six to eight selectors, and an auctioneer to dispose of a cargo. The scene was described as follows:

> The dock is usually filled with buyers and their trucks, and in a few hours the steamer's hold is empty. A cargo of 32,000 bunches, one of the largest that ever arrived here, was disposed of last week in ten hours. The auctioneer stands on the steamer's bridge, and the buyers crowd close to him. A sort of endless chain runs from the hold to the pier. Bunch after bunch is laid in the chain—an arrangement that has been in operation for only about three months—and as each bunch is lifted out an expert, who is known as a "selector," and who is as skillful in his trade as a tea-taster is in his, runs his eye over it and pronounces it in quality a first, second, third, or "dock," and then it is quickly loaded, according to grade in a waiting wagon.[3]

A stem with seven hands or more was considered a first, of six hands a second, and of five a third.[4] The "docks" were ripe or soft fruit, unsuitable for sale by the commission merchants. They were sold to street peddlers "who swarm about with their carts, and are looking for bargains."[5]

It took some capital and many experiments to learn the best method of handling bananas as they made their journey from the plantation to the ship, from the ship to the railroad to the warehouse, and ultimately to the retail store. Cut and shipped green, the fruit had to be allowed to ripen slowly so that it reached the consumer in salable form. Bananas that were either too green or too

brown were unappealing to customers; the optimal stage of ripening was a clear, bright yellow. Wholesale dealers in New York City in
the 1890s had to hold bananas for four or five days to ripen before
sale in the city. Those that were to be sent any distance were kept
green as long as possible by keeping them cool.[6]

Prior to the development of an organized distribution system, inland grocers who ordered bananas from importing companies did
so at their own risk.[7] The fruit changed hands many times between
the plantation and the retail store, and extremes of temperature or
rough handling could easily damage the fruit along the way. Even
perfectly ripening fruit had to be distributed promptly to shopkeepers to allow sufficient time for it to be sold to the customer. In
response to these problems, United Fruit organized the Fruit Dispatch Company in 1898 to handle the distribution and sale of their
bananas and other tropical imports.[8]

Banana distribution companies searched for ways to control the
speed of ripening of the fruit to ensure that it reached the customer
in good condition. Refrigerated or heated steamship holds, railroad
cars, and warehouses were designed especially for bananas. With
the ripening process reasonably under control, retail stores could
be kept supplied with salable fruit at all times. An article in the 1905
U.S. Department of Agriculture Year Book noted that:

> there has been a gradual evolution of special transportation fa-
> cilities from the box car, the pony refrigerators, and the slow ex-
> press or boat service, with their irregular schedules, of forty
> years ago. The fast fruit-train service, the fruit-express car, the
> refrigerator car lines, the special fruit boats, the refrigerator
> compartments on shipboard, and the development of cold-
> storage warehouses as a link in the chain of distribution have
> brought together the producer and the consumer in the most
> distant parts of the United States and Canada.[9]

As distribution networks were established, fruit-import companies
relied less upon direct dockside sales and more upon distribution

centers in the interior cities. The Fruit Dispatch Company initially set up distributing divisions in twenty-one northern cities, including Buffalo, Chicago, Denver, Saint Louis, Montreal, and Pittsburgh.[10] By 1923 there were forty-nine branches and over four hundred employees.[11] Twelve years later the company had expanded to include fifty-two branch offices that sold bananas by the carload to jobbers.[12] Orders were telegraphed or telephoned to offices at the ports of entry before the cargo was discharged, making loading and distribution more efficient.

Once the bananas reached major metropolitan centers by ship and railroad freight car, they were stored in special ripening warehouses with separate rooms kept at the different temperatures that would either hasten or retard the ripening process, according to orders received from retail stores.[13] The Fruit Dispatch Company provided plans for these warehouses and technical advice for their construction.

In the 1930s ethylene gas was introduced to produce uniformity in ripening and to speed up slow ripening fruit. The gas intensified the coloration of the peel and accelerated the ripening of the pulp. Although the gas was an anaesthetic, the Fruit Dispatch Company assured warehouse workers that "in the very dilute amounts used for ripening" it "does no harm to workmen."[14] This information was based on 110 ripening tests performed by the United Fruit Company Research Department in respiration chambers. An additional 134 ripening tests were carried out in small ripening rooms, and larger rooms were used to prove results on a commercial scale.

In the 1990s the major grocery store chains have their own warehouses with ripening rooms. Safeway, a grocery store chain in Maryland and the District of Columbia, has six huge storage facilities at their distribution center in Upper Marlborough, Maryland, housing 2,000 cardboard cases of bananas per room, 100 banana fingers to the box. Another large chain, Giant, has thirty rooms at a warehouse in Lanham, Maryland. Each room accommodates about 900 cases of bananas, and holds bananas at a different stage of the ripening process. The pressurized rooms use humidity, temperature, and a small dose of ethylene gas that mimic conditions in the tropics to control the ripening time. The bananas are tested periodically until they are ready to be trucked to the supermarkets.[15]

Field servicers were sent out to help banana jobbers with various problems in an attempt to avoid losses due to bruising and premature ripening. As the distribution system narrowed from shipload to boxcar load to individual order, the banana jobbers were responsible for breaking down the shipments to single stems of fruit

Banana crate, *Story of the Banana*, Education Department (Boston: United Fruit, 1925), 40.

for delivery to individual grocery stores. Special crates of various sizes and design were devised for this purpose. Returnable crates were constructed of oak slats with a burlap bag suspended inside and tied so that the stem with its hands of bananas could not be bruised. Nonreturnable crates made of lighter slats held a paper bag in which the fruit was packed in hay or straw. Another packing device was a cylindrical cardboard drum strengthened with wooden

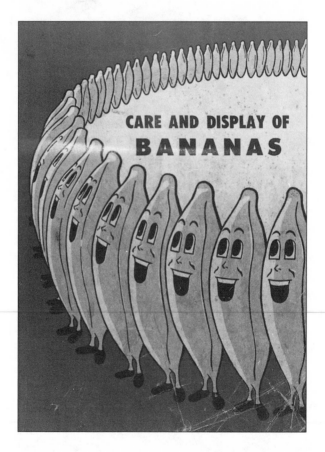

Care and Display of Bananas, Fruit Dispatch Company
Dealer Service Department (1955).

bottoms and hoops.[16] In the 1930s wholesalers experimented with cutting ripe hands of bananas off the stem and packing them in wooden boxes for distribution. These boxes nested together, making them easier to return, as they did not take up much space.[17]

Dealer servicemen gave advice on retail merchandising of bananas in the stores. They prepared window displays and provided advertising copy and other tips on marketing the fruit to the consumer.[18] Grocers were encouraged to display bananas on the stalk in their store windows or other areas where they would be readily seen. This was not always a successful sales ploy as shown in Sinclair Lewis's novel *Main Street,* in which he described a grocery store display window with "black overripe bananas and lettuce on which a cat was sleeping." In the winter the fruit had to be protected from drafts of cold air and the bunches covered with paper bags or other wrappings at night in case the temperature in the store got too low.[19] The stalk with the bunches of bananas still on it was suspended upside down and the grocer cut off the hands of fruit for customers with a special banana knife to avoid tearing the skin and exposing the pulp. The knife looked something like a linoleum cutter with a wooden handle and curved blade with the cutting edge on the inside curve.[20]

As self-service grocery stores and supermarkets proliferated in the mid-twentieth century, the hands were cut from the stalk in advance and set out on tables or counters for customers to select for themselves. Left to their own devices, customers were apt to break apart the hands of bananas to purchase two or three at a time. This left unappealing clusters or single fingers of fruit, often with the skin split open and unsalable. The loose bananas and damaged fruit was either marked down in price or discarded.

The Fruit Dispatch Company experimented to see whether it was possible to persuade the customer to purchase the entire hand, and therefore, it was hoped, to consume more bananas. Some grocers bound six or eight individual fingers with gummed tape to simulate a bunch to be sold at full price.[21] One merchandising study that banded the fruit with paper tape on which was marked the weight and price found that large hands did not sell as well as smaller quantities.[22]

In the mid-1960s, hands of bananas were wrapped in a sleeve of heat-shrinkable film at a central warehouse. The wrap protected the hands from bruising, prevented the customer from removing individual fruit, and provided a surface for the label. This method had a "potential savings of 43 cents per forty-pound box when compared with the typical method of tape banding bananas at the retail store."[23] It worked well for the retailer but in many places customers rebelled, preferring to choose their own fresh fruit rather than purchase them packaged. Most supermarkets in the 1990s have returned to displays of unpackaged hands of bananas, and food stores, such as the Safeway chain in the Washington, D.C., area provide special little paper bags with handles for marked-down single fingers or overripe fruit. The white bag is printed with a picture of a yellow banana with the peel pulled down halfway. Over it is printed "Ripe Bananas—Ready for Eating and Cooking," and a recipe for banana bread, one use for overripe bananas.

In the 1930s United Fruit briefly experimented with shipping hands of bananas in wooden boxes rather than on the stalk, but the experiment failed owing to the high cost of boxing.[24] The first boxes used in the experiment were efficient to transport but held the heat generated by ripening bananas, causing problems with uneven and premature ripening in transit. Their use was abandoned until the 1950s.

A 1955 marketing research report released by the Agricultural Marketing Service of the U.S. Department of Agriculture noted that the banana was still "one of the few perishable products handled without packaging between the point of production and the wholesale outlet." According to the report, distributors were becoming increasingly interested in improved methods for receiving, ripening, and packing bananas for retail trade in order to cut losses from bruising and deterioration.[25] Fruit companies again experimented with boxing hands of bananas at the plantation or the exporting port, rather than transporting the fruit on the stalk and packaging it at the port of arrival. The usual practice was to leave rejected bananas that had either come loose from the stem or were deemed too small or too large for the United States and Canadian markets. Innovations in cardboard boxing and the establishment of processing factories in the banana-growing regions cut down on the enormous waste of fruit.

Chiquita Brands International found a market niche for the individual bananas that become detached from the hand during harvesting. An advertisement to the restaurant trade in 1991 offered "Chef Singles—10 pounds of individual Chiquita bananas prepacked in the tropics in sturdy, easy-to-use boxes."[26] Dole also advertised ten-pound boxes of single bananas, assuring food service managers that "you can serve your customers fresh bananas at the peak of ripeness any day of the week, any meal of the day" without having to bother with breaking up the fruit into individual servings.[27]

The creation of a sturdy cardboard box with air holes and built-in handles is attributed to B. C. D'Antoni, an engineer with the Standard Fruit Company.[28] Cardboard boxes eliminated many steps in processing, handling, and shipping since the fruit remained in the container from the plantation to the retail store, reducing labor as well as bruising. Standard Fruit built three box factories in Honduras and one in Costa Rica.[29] The rest of the banana industry soon converted to shipping fruit in cartons.[30] In 1962 the U.S. Department of Commerce changed its reports from the number of stems of bananas imported to hundred-weight of fruit.[31] As boxing became the standard method of transporting bananas, hanging stems displaying hands of fruit disappeared from grocery store windows, although for a while vertical cardboard displays of individual hands continued to mimic the familiar banana stalk.

The cardboard banana boxes also have a re-use value. The Capital Area Community Food Bank in Washington, D.C., for example, uses them to store and transport surplus food collected from grocery stores and other businesses. Available food is even measured in terms of numbers of banana boxes.

In addition to improvements in transportation, handling, and storage of bananas, advertising has had a great deal to do with modern food choices. Advertising is used to convince the consumer to purchase surpluses at the highest possible price. Americans are faced with a wide range of products when they go food shopping; advertising develops brand loyalty and may help people decide what to buy. Bananas were introduced into the United States at the same time as the development of the popular press, widespread literacy, and the appearance of women's magazines and a multitude of cookbooks. At the turn of the century, an expanding middle class used food as a means of defining itself by imitating the preferences of the rich and rejecting the hallmarks of the poor such as pork, brown bread, thick soups, and dried fruit pies.[32] Women no longer learned to cook from their mothers and grandmothers as new nutritional standards incorporating vitamins and calories rejected and disparaged older ways. Young women turned to authorities outside the home, such as the dietitians and scientists represented in advertising, to learn new ways of preparing and serving food for their families.

Bananas were the perfect new food for the rising middle class. Advertising before 1923 featured the banana "not only as a luxurious fruit but as a pure, nutritious food, suitable alike for the rich and the poor."[33] The fruit companies were ready with plenty of scientific advice and recipes to stimulate sales. The Fruit Dispatch Company was responsible for national advertising and promotional efforts of United Fruit as well as the logistics of banana transportation.

In 1929 the Fruit Dispatch Company hired consultants to prepare a scientific market research brief that examined the current advertising campaign, interviewed consumers, and recommended future advertising emphases.[34] The consultants surveyed 8,500 consumers and 1,741 retail dealers, and visited 341 institutions including tearooms, soda fountains, hospitals, boarding houses, restaurants, and clubs. The survey was conducted in twenty-eight cities of varying size in Massachusetts, Georgia, Ohio, and Iowa and included both suburban and farming communities in adjacent areas.

Survey results indicated that the advertising emphasis on low price and the tropical origin of the banana should be revised, and that a new advertising campaign be directed at the middle class with emphasis on style, quality, and the health benefits of eating bananas. "This will not hurt the poor who now buy, but will actually influence the potential better-class market whose limit is far from reached." In addition, the children's market had still greater potential: "The work of the Educational and Medical departments of the United Fruit Company is now bearing fruit in the wholesale endorsement of ripe bananas for growing children by the medical profession." The survey also found that there was a tendency for adults to stop eating bananas as they reached the age of forty or fifty, and recommended that this age group be encouraged to eat more bananas as a protective and vitalizing food.

In response to the survey, the advertising budget for 1930 was doubled from that of 1929 and advertisements were placed in ten national magazines. The advertising campaign for 1930 included style and appetite appeal along with the news that bananas "are a delicious food that is good for something as well as good to eat." The new campaign offered a banana book "brimful of useful recipes, menus, and serving suggestions prepared by nutrition experts. Send coupon for your copy. Be among the first to benefit by the new knowledge of the banana." Sample advertising copy read as follows:

Vitality in every bite of this Natural Food . . . that's why bananas belong in the daily diet. A vital addition to the diet. That's what nutrition experts are calling the banana. For this natural food-fruit abounds in important food materials. No fewer than three vitamins—for health and growth. Energy-building *carbohydrates*, too. And valuable stores of *minerals*, so necessary for body tone. . . . Add to all this a ripe banana's quick, easy digestibility and fine, mellow flavor . . . its handiness to peel and eat any-

The
NEW ·
BANANA

Breaking the connection to Latin America, *The New Banana* (New York: United Fruit, Fruit Dispatch Company, 1931).

where, at any hour . . . its price—always an inviting one. Then you'll see why prominent food authorities are now urging that *bananas belong* on every family table.[35]

To appeal to middle-class consumers, 1930 advertising copy showed father in a business suit going off to work, two well-dressed women having lunch in a department store restaurant, and a woman being served breakfast in bed by a uniformed maid.

The 1929 consumer survey found that households with children ate more bananas, so many of the marketing efforts in the following years targeted children. Marketing strategies provided materials to classroom teachers, including nutrition information, recipes, films, pictures to color, sheet music, maps, and geography lessons. Teach children to like bananas, and the children would ask mother for them and, in addition, grow up to serve bananas to their own families.

The Fruit Dispatch Company pioneered industry-sponsored educational materials for public schools and in 1929 established a separate Education Department in addition to the Advertising De-

Boy Scouts cooking bananas, *About Bananas,* Education Department (United Fruit, 1936).

partment.[36] Corporate logos and advertisements in the classrooms in the 1990s are not new. Between 1930 and 1955, the Education Department produced more than thirty-five different printed educational materials for classroom use.

In 1939 United Fruit Company's Home Economics Department produced a teacher's manual with the title *A Study of the Banana: Its Everyday Use and Food Value.* The manual provided more detailed information for the teacher and included additional topics such as "suggested ways of preparing and serving bananas and ten simple meal-planning suggestions."[37] The manual covered the food value of the fruit, its germ-proof wrapper, and the importance of bananas to physicians in combating nutritional disorders. Bananas were presented as a "highly desirable" food for the elderly as well as a valuable addition to the diet of young children. A photograph of a classroom in Sublette, Kansas, dated April 1941, includes a poster on one wall that reads "Bananas and Milk: Good Teammates!"[38]

In the 1950s a set of nine student lessons were available for varying grade levels with accompanying teacher worksheets plus three films for classroom use. The color film, "Journey to Bananaland," was in such demand in 1954 that the number of prints was increased from 214 to 314.[39] Between 1955 and 1962, nearly 15 million pieces of banana literature were published by United Fruit Company for students in the elementary grades through high school. These also were sent to schools around the world.[40]

In 1962 United Fruit provided teachers with four-page student lesson sheets on bananas and the countries of Middle America, a folder of banana recipes, a wall chart, a sound motion picture, a filmstrip, and an eight-page teacher's manual on how to get and use these aids. This material was recommended for geography, history, social studies, health and nutrition, elementary and general science and biology classes.[41] The 1969 educational kit, marketed for the classroom at $4.00 apiece, contained thirty copies of the booklet "People Like Bananas," a fifty-frame filmstrip with the title "The Musa Finds a Market," plus an illustrated script, a complete teacher's guide, and suggestions for related classroom activities.[42]

United Fruit also sought to expand the market for bananas through the school lunchroom. In 1967 the company distributed 90,000 full-color illustrated recipe cards for Chiquita banana and peanut butter sandwiches to schools throughout the United States, promoting the sandwiches as a lunch-time treat.[43]

Early United Fruit Company promotional efforts recommended banana consumption in general. Bananas were convenient, delicious, and nutritious, and United Fruit advertising often focused on the healthful aspects of the fruit, an important source of vitamins, minerals, and energy. By the 1940s, in the face of competition from other large fruit-import corporations, United Fruit came up with the notion of brand-name bananas. Identifying the importing agent by brand name promised quality and status and fit with similar marketing strategies for other packaged brand-name foods at the time.

In 1944 United Fruit, planning ahead to the return of its ships to the Caribbean banana trade at the end of the war, hired Dik Browne (better known today as creator of the Hagar the Horrible cartoon strip) to create a cartoon character based on the Latin American singer and movie star of the 1930s and '40s, Carmen Miranda.[44] Chiquita Banana first appeared in a 1945 technicolor movie advertisement with the title "Miss Chiquita Banana's Beauty Treatment," in which she burst into song to revive an exhausted housewife. In it Chiquita advises, "You'll find by eating fruit you'll have a more beautiful appearance and complexion," and "a daily dose of bananas will help you look perfection."[45]

Next, Chiquita became part of an educational campaign to promote two basic ideas: bananas taste better if eaten when their peels have brown or "sugar" spots; and bananas should be allowed to ripen at room temperature, "never in the refrigerator." This was in the postwar era when many American households had a refrigerator for the first time.[46] Chiquita wore a bowl of fruit on her head and her antirefrigeration calypso song, written by Garth Montgomery and Len MacKenzie, transcended advertising to become a popular hit recorded by musicians such as Patty Clayton, Xavier Cugat, and the King Sisters. The Chiquita jingle was so popular that it

"Chiquita Banana" sheet music (Maxwell-Wirges
Publications, 1945, printed 1950).

was played on the radio 376 times in one day, and Chiquita was
named "the girl we'd most like to share a foxhole with" by American enlisted men.[47] United Fruit even provided copies of the sheet
music to schools to build "interest in bananas among many millions
of future food purchasers."[48]

Americans learned that bananas should "never" be stored in the
refrigerator, despite the fact that the fruit was shipped under refrigeration and that home refrigeration, while blackening the skin,
halts the ripening process so that bananas keep longer. It was a mar-

keting success for United Fruit in that housewives believed that they had to use the bananas they bought more quickly than was actually necessary. The campaign was so successful that food writers for popular magazines repeated the caution.[49] Many people in the United States continue to believe that they should never put their bananas in the refrigerator, despite occasional advice to the contrary.[50]

United Fruit created the individual banana label in 1962.[51] Small blue paper seals with a picture of Chiquita Banana were affixed to banana clusters in the tropics and United Fruit Company advertised heavily to create demand for brand-name bananas. This changed the business from that of selling a commodity to that of selling a branded, identifiable product.[52] Chiquita-labeled fruit was soon selling at premium prices with the promise of superior quality.[53] Consumer comments in 1964 after two years of the new program included "these are the bananas we have seen on TV," and "these have labels on the peel; they must be good."[54] Independent market research organizations found that the brand-name bananas consistently sold at higher prices than unbranded bananas, and that there was a high level of brand awareness and acceptance among consumers.[55]

Chiquita Banana was resurrected for her "twenty-first birthday" in 1966, and Elsa Miranda, no relation to Carmen Miranda, was chosen to represent Chiquita. She appeared on national television and radio programs, gave interviews to newspapers and magazines, and toured the country to promote banana sales.[56] In honor of the occasion, United Fruit published "21 Chiquita Banana Classics," a collection of recipes that included banana quick bread, fruit shakes, banana jewel ring, banana fritters, and banana cream pie.[57] Both Butterick and McCall's published Chiquita Banana Costume Patterns for women and girls including a dress and hat, and Betty Crocker developed a Chiquita Banana Cake and Frosting Mix.[58] The Chiquita advertising jingle was once again a familiar tune in American homes. On May 3, 1995, the NBC television show "A Word from Our Sponsor" included "Chiquita Banana" among the all-time top-ten best advertising jingles.

In addition to Chiquita Banana, advertising in the 1960s urged consumers to eat bananas "for goodness' sake," promoted bananas as ideal baby food with high vitamin content, and appealed to the diet conscious with the claim that a banana had fewer calories than cottage cheese and was without "a trace of cholesterol."[59] Banana advertisements in the 1970s featured celebrities such as Milton Berle and Bugs Bunny singing the Chiquita song from inside a banana. Company advertising returned to a health pitch in 1983 with a television advertisement set in a grocery store with a mother shopping for a low sodium, high-fiber multivitamin. She selects a jar from the shelf that contains little bananas. The voice over advises "take one a day."[60]

In addition to a brand name, adhesive labels have also been used to promote the use of bananas. In conjunction with the Nabisco Company, one-inch square stickers representing cereal boxes appeared on bananas in the 1980s. There were three different stickers promoting Shredded Wheat, Shredded Wheat 'n' Bran, and Spoon Size Shredded Wheat. At the top of each label was the caption "Try me on" or "I'm great on" and each showed a bowl of cereal next to a bunch of bananas. Kellogg's cereals offered coupons for free bananas and promoted them with banana stickers that read "See Kellogg's Offer for Free Bananas." Jello stickers have also shared the banana peel advertising space.

Chiquita has used sticky labels that read "Take Me To Work," "Potassium Rich," "One A Day For Five A Day," "#1 Fruit Snack," and "Take One In The Morning," to promote greater banana consumption. There was even a Christmas sticker with a striped red and green border like a candy cane that read "The Perfect Stocking Stuffer." In 1992 Chiquita Brands International, the successor to United Fruit Company, spent almost $20 million a year on television and magazine advertising to convince shoppers that bananas with the Chiquita sticker were somehow worth more than those with other brands.[61] Today banana stickers are collectors items with special banana sticker albums available over the Internet.

In 1994 for the fiftieth anniversary of Chiquita, the company produced stickers that pictured past incarnations of the singing ba-

Chiquita Banana seal on a
magnet.

nana, and sponsored a contest to select a new Miss Chiquita. Elizabeth Testa, an actress from Syracuse, New York, was chosen to travel
around the country handing out bananas while wearing a bowl of
fruit on her head.[62]

By 1966 other banana producers were also promoting brand-
name bananas.[63] United Fruit countered with a defensive advertisement in *Parents Magazine* that showed a hand of bananas with two
blue Chiquita stickers. The text read:

> "Can You Ever Get A Bad One? Can Miss America ever get a
> run in her stocking?" Of course, she can. And that occasional
> thing known as a "bum banana" can happen to us, too. Let's
> face it. We're not dealing with some machine that turns out cars
> or soap. We're dealing with nature. And things can happen. A
> banana with a defect can somehow slip by. Or a Chiquita Ba-
> nana can spend the weekend on a store counter. Or a grape-
> fruit can fall on it. Or a customer can prod where she should
> have patted. But, you'll have to admit, a bum Chiquita Brand
> Banana is no everyday thing. We work too hard and care too

much for that to happen. Nobody else does. But, then, nobody else has the nerve to run an ad like this, either."[64]

Chiquita, Dole, Bonita, Del Monte, Darien, Reyban, Turbana, Bananacol, Del Lago, Sura, Sunisa, Fyffes, and Lacuna stickers all show up from time to time in the Washington, D.C., area. As grocery store checkout lines became computerized, banana labels began to include the number 4011 as a memory aid to cashiers who entered the code number of each fruit and vegetable as it was being weighed. Other fruit and vegetable producers followed suit, brand-labeling apples, oranges, tomatoes, and pears. In the late 1990s, large grocery chains such as Stop & Shop affixed their own coded labels on non-brand-name bananas and other produce.

Most people, however, tend to ignore the brand names on fruit since there is usually no choice between brands at any one time. The tactic may even backfire at times when consumers refuse to purchase fruit imported from certain countries or by certain corporations. Unlike the tropical countries where there are many types of banana, the North American market generally receives Cavendish bananas and the consumer is unaware of any difference between company brands.

United Fruit tried offering gift premiums in conjunction with banana purchases in the 1960s. The first major promotion in October 1964 promised live miniature rose bushes in exchange for four Chiquita Brand seals and fifty cents. It was hoped that this promotion would boost customer awareness and sales of Chiquita bananas. The campaign covered forty major United States markets and included intensive television and related in-store advertising.[65] The company soon switched to more product-related goods such as "Best of the Bunch Banana Beach Bags" promoted by disc jockeys on 109 Mutual Broadcasting stations. The blue bags embossed with a golden crown of bananas and the words "Best of the Bunch" were given away as prizes to contestants who wrote banana lyrics to the tune "Clementine."[66] Other promotional items have included a Chiquita Banana pup tent, a Chiquita Banana sleeping bag-comforter, a Chiquita Banana windbreaker, Chiquita Banana breakfast bowl and spoon, and a Chiquita Banana backpack.[67]

In the 1990s bananas were advertised as a food rather than a fruit, taking advantage of renewed consumer interest in physical fitness and nutrition. Television and print advertisements called bananas "quite possibly the world's perfect food."[68] Images of mountain bikers, small children, and grandparents were used to make the point that good nutrition was not just for athletes.[69] One advertisement, however, harkened back to the original Chiquita Banana advertisement of 1945 that targeted women's concerns for their appearance. It showed a vanity table, cluttered with cosmetics and a banana peel, with the caption: "True beauty lies beneath the skin."[70]

Chiquita Brands International also experimented with providing a toll-free telephone number and a medical expert to answer questions about bananas, offering a "Chiquita Value Plan" to help Americans eat better. Callers were asked to provide the age and sex of family members and the amount of the family budget spent on food. In return they were promised a personalized menu plan and shopping guide. Critics charged that Chiquita was soliciting demographics that could be combined with other databases and were concerned that Chiquita might be tempted to share the information with other companies. In addition they pointed out that there were only two menu plans, one economic and the other for higher incomes, a far cry from the personalized service promised by the company. The shopping guide suggested that consumers purchase seven pounds of Chiquita bananas each week in comparison with much smaller quantities of other fruit.[71]

A smaller variety of banana is finding a new niche in our eating habits. Despite United Fruit Company claims to the contrary, Weight Watchers recommends only a half a banana per serving. Chiquita Brands began test marketing smaller bananas called Chiquita Jr. in 1992, targeting children and diet-conscious adults.[72] Smaller bananas are popular because it is easier to consume an entire fruit than to try to save half and have it turn brown or to share it with someone else. Smaller bananas also fit better into lunch boxes. After years of rejecting bananas less than nine inches in length, the seven-inch banana is finding a place in the American supermarket.[73]

At the end of an intensive century of advertising, the question still remains: are advertisements effective? They can promote short-term sales but can they really build customer loyalty to brand names?[74] Particularly for something like fruit, brand names are difficult to make meaningful. United Fruit Company, now Chiquita Brands International, has lost market share to other North American and Central American companies while the people of the United States continue to eat surprising numbers of bananas. Bananas remain the cheapest fruit in the supermarket, representing a triumph in distribution as well as of advertising and marketing programs.

5

PERIL AND PANACEA

GROWING INTEREST IN NEW information about nutrition and domestic science completely changed the way people thought of their world, especially about what they ate. Bananas were introduced into the United States at roughly the same time as discoveries were being made concerning calories, germs, and vitamins. Changing notions about sanitation, diet, and disease incorporated the newly available fruit, absorbing bananas into American myth and folklore as well as into scientific circles as both peril and panacea.

Fresh fruit had a marginal place in the American diet in the nineteenth century. The adage that "fruit is golden in the morning, silver at noon, and leaden at night" led many cookbook and etiquette book writers to promote fruit as appropriate for breakfast.[1] Before much was known about nutrition, some believed that "fruits do not take an important place as nutrients. They belong rather among the luxuries, and yet, as an agreeable stimulant to digestion, they occupy a front rank."[2] It was widely known that "fruits, when eaten under-ripe or over-ripe, disarrange the digestive organs."[3] The laxative properties of fruit were understood long before nutrition became a science.

Maria Parola, the well-known housekeeping authority, assured her readers in 1882 that "fresh fruits are very necessary to perfect health. They must be ripe and sound to be entirely healthful. Unripe and decaying fruit causes a great amount of sickness and death every year in our large cities, where it is sold at low prices on the streets."[4] Apples, Parola suggested, were the most useful of fruits but "figs, dates, and bananas, either fresh or preserved, are very healthful, nutritious fruits." Mrs. Lincoln, another contemporary cookbook author, suggested that fresh fruit could be "a great saving of time and work, give a pleasing variety to bills of fare, and be above all a great promoter of health, if people would use ripe fruit abundantly in its season at their tables (not between meals). With the markets bountifully supplied with many varieties of fruit, it is to be regretted that it cannot be found at every table at least once a day."[5] In response, Catherine Owen protested in *The Homemaker* that

> many good people speaking of the lack of thrift among the poor point to their neglect of fruit as a cheap and more wholesome food than meat. Cheaper I do not think it could be, except on the rare occasion of a glut in the market, for it will not take the place of all other things, and if a woman has but twenty-five cents for her dinner expenses, meat, vegetables, etc., she would find it difficult to squeeze more than a quarter of an orange, half a dozen grapes, or part of a banana for each person, unless meat be left out.[6]

Owen went on to say that "bananas are sometimes very cheap, and they take the place of meat better than any other fruit, being it is said, very nutritious."

Nineteenth-century Americans believed that fruit was dangerous for young children. This belief, also prevalent throughout Europe, can be traced to Galen, a Greek physician of the second century A.D.[7] Infantile diarrhea, frequent in the summertime, was a great killer and reinforced the fear of fresh fruit known to be a laxative. In 1867 American mothers were assured that this "prejudice arise[s] not from the injurious qualities of ripe sound fruit of any kind, but because children will not discriminate between that which is ripe and that which is nearly so, and because they are likely to eat fruits of all kinds to excess."[8] If children were to be served bananas, the fruit "should always be cooked, unless they are very ripe and the skins quite black."[9]

Other household arbiters held that children were not to eat fruit or fruit juice, other than orange juice, until after the age of two and a half. A young child's diet should consist of "plenty of milk, a roasted potato once a day, oatmeal or some other simple cereal *without sugar,* a little beefsteak or bouillon or beef-juice three times a week, stale bread and plain crackers, which the average child under two years can safely eat, and know no longing after such doubtful articles as vegetables and fruits."[10] It is a wonder that so many people survived childhood.

Forbidden fruit figured frequently in moral tales about children who were dishonest, stealing from an orchard or the table, and children spent their pennies on fruit, just as today they spend their allowance on candy. An 1885 editorial asked the New York City police to enforce the laws against street vendors who sold unripe and rotten fruit:

> The victims of this evil traffic are generally children, who in their eagerness for fruit and their ignorance of the danger in eating it when in an unwholesome condition, are liberal patrons, as long as their pennies last, of whatever unscrupulous vendors may offer that is within their means. . . . Children do not know that when one end of a banana, or one side of a melon, peach, or cherry is rotten, the whole of the article is unfit to be eaten, but the wretch who sells it does know and the policeman should."[11]

In her recollections of growing up in Maine in the 1890s, Mary Ellen Chase wrote of the cargo of a coastal schooner from New York: "Most remarkable of all her goods in those relatively fruitless days

Selling bananas from a wagon, *U.F. Report* 1 (April, 1951).

were crates of oranges, two kegs of white grapes, packed in sawdust, and—most wonderful to relate!—a huge bunch of bananas in a long, slatted frame." Chase went on to say that "We were all excessively fond of them [bananas], but since they were tacitly recognized as an indulgence and since the price of them in the village store, at least of enough to supply our family, was prohibitive, we had never completely satisfied our desire." The Chase children were the envy of the neighborhood for days. "I can yet feel the stilling of my heart when he [father] handed down to me, who waited below with outstretched apron, five, six, eight, twelve bananas, when he proposed that we should treat our friends."[12]

In the on-going debate as to when a banana was ripe and fit to eat, a 1916 newspaper article stated that

> children under three years of age do not chew their food thoroughly; they bolt it. For this reason they should not have bananas to eat uncooked. Bananas are nutritious, but they are an

indigestible food unless they are well masticated. They are more easily digested when cooked than when eaten raw."[13]

A 1918 magazine article suggested that while the fruit should not be "the main component of the child's dietary . . . can compete well with other fruits, and is decidedly to be preferred to candies."[14] An article in *Scientific American* pointed out that "a yellow banana is not necessarily a ripe banana and if consumed raw while it still has a green cast to the yellow color, as is frequently done by children on the streets, the availability of its carbohydrates is comparatively low and the effect on the child's digestive system injurious."[15] Bananas were not to be eaten raw until flecked with brown "sugar" spots.

One magazine writer suggested that the idea of indigestibility might have come from "the strange attraction which some children have for the inside of the peel, and for the long white strings of pulpy tissue which often adhere to the banana from the peeling," and recommended scraping the banana before eating as the "strings" might not agree with everyone.[16] A decade later an article in the *Ladies Home Journal* queried, "Do you know that the 'strings' sometimes left on peeled bananas are indigestible? This is why a banana which is to be eaten by a child should first be scraped."[17]

In the late nineteenth century, a major domestic reform movement swept the country that promoted the elevation of traditional household responsibilities to the status of a profession, in which all the new resources of science and technology were applied to the improvement and more efficient management of the home.[18] Many middle-class women adopted into their housework the new scientific principles, variously known as "scientific housekeeping," "home science," "progressive housekeeping," and more widely, "domestic science."[19]

The late-nineteenth-century fairs provided opportunities to demonstrate and teach these new developments. During the Columbian Exposition in Chicago in 1893, proponents of the new domestic science ran a demonstration kitchen; it served lunches with menus that specified calculated food values to demonstrate to the public the meaning of the new terms "proteids, carbohydrates, calories, and the fact there are scientific principles underlying nutrition."[20]

The American Home Economics Association was founded in 1909 with initial research topics such as the digestibility of foods; calorie needs and the energy relationships of fat, protein, and carbohydrate; and the significance of inorganic elements in the body.[21] During the next ten years, housewives were deluged with articles in newspapers and magazines about the relationship of nutrition and diet to health, and were exhorted to produce three "protective" meals a day for a healthy family. In the 1920s and 1930s research expanded to vitamins and minerals, especially iron, calcium, and the vitamins A, B, and C, with emphasis on the measurement of these nutrients in food and in the body. Most important of all were the recommendations for optimal growth and health.[22]

In 1882 Robert Koch laid the basis for the germ theory of disease and furnished a rational basis for practical preventive measures.[23] The identification of bacteria by Joseph Lister, Louis Pasteur, and Robert Koch, and the discovery of the relationship of germs to disease, had initially led many physicians to believe that all disease was caused by germs.[24] Wives and mothers found themselves responsible for the health of family members who might come upon deadly germs in the new indoor bathrooms or in the food they ate. The preface of one home economics textbook stated that:

At present it is necessary for those expecting to become housewives to understand the elementary phases of a number of sciences, most prominent among which are chemistry and bacteriology. The relation of microorganisms to household affairs is now felt to be one of the most important phases of domestic science. The present work is designed for all interested in household affairs, including not only students in domestic science but all housewives who are interested in keeping their homes in the best and most healthful condition.[25]

This connection of germs to disease was made more frightening by twentieth-century advertisers who dwelt on the dangers of unseen

The Food Value of the Banana, Research Department
(Boston: United Fruit, 1928).

germs to sell everything from bananas to bathroom cleansers and
refrigerators.

To encourage nervous mothers to purchase bananas, promoters
emphasized that the fruit came "with its own germ-proof wrapper."[26] Indeed, "a banana, properly handled is uncontaminated by
dirt and pathogenic germs even if purchased from the pushcart in
our congested streets."[27] An article in *Good Housekeeping* assured

American Medical Association seal
of approval, *Radio Bound for Banana
Land,* J. Mace Andress and Julia E.
Dickson, Education Department
(Boston: United Fruit, 1932), 3.

women readers that "nature has given us in the banana a sanitary,
sealed package containing a food which includes all the elements
of an ideal foodstuff."[28] The *Ladies Home Journal* warned that bananas should always be cut rather than torn from the bunch because "as long as the skin of a banana is unbroken it is a sterile

food."[29] The American Medical Association also recommended bananas as "A Fruit in a Sterile Package," citing the work of Dr. E. M. Bailey who had "made extensive bacteriologic examinations of the fruits in different stages of maturation."[30] In 1926 a pamphlet entitled "The Food Value of the Banana" noted that "the banana is hermetically sealed in its skin. This is an important health protection from dust, mould, flies, and dirty hands."[31]

The science of nutrition gained prominence during World War I when various food stuffs were rationed. As patriotic households were urged to give up meat and wheat on specified days, women needed to learn about alternative meal preparation. Bananas were promoted as a nutritious substitute even though they were not always readily available owing to loss of banana freighters to the war effort. Ten years later, an editorial in the *Journal of the American Medical Association* noted that prejudices about the digestibility of bananas "are gradually being broken down with the progress in the experimental study of nutrition," and that bananas were now included even in infants' diets.[32]

Turn-of-the-century dietary standards were based on calorie levels and the balance of protein, fat, and carbohydrates. Fruit and vegetables were not considered very important to a healthy diet. Dietary scientists estimated the number of calories needed to be consumed daily by men, women, and children, and began to test all food stuffs for their nutritional components. Standards were developed for people by age, sex, and activity. Homemakers were encouraged to count the calories for all the members of their families to be sure that each person ate the proper amount. The initial emphasis was upon eating a sufficient number of calories rather than worrying about consuming too many calories. Being underweight was perceived as more of a health threat than overweight. Large bananas have approximately a hundred calories each and were "regarded not as a fruit to eat casually but as a substantial food.[33] The *Journal of the American Medical Association* noted that "it is well to bear in mind in the case of the banana that its caloric value is very high, in fact higher than that of any other common fruit in its natural state."[34] In 1929 the Education Department of United Fruit Com-

pany published the fifth edition of *The Story of the Banana*. The fruit
was praised as

> one of the most convenient fruits to use. It may be readily
> served in many ways and its flavor blends agreeably with those
> of other fruits and foods. When combined with other fresh
> fruits and the leafy vegetables, it supplies the needed Calories.
> These facts are appreciated not only by housewives and hospital
> dietitians, but by those in charge of hotel dining rooms, restau-
> rants and school cafeterias.[35]

Food and medicine have been linked "ever since human beings began viewing ingestion and fasting as instruments of health and pu-
rity."[36] The discovery of vitamins confirmed the connection and the
way people thought about food, giving it medicinal qualities. In
1906 an English chemist, Frederick Gowland Hopkins, studying de-
ficiency diseases such as beriberi, scurvy, and rickets, suggested that
some things the body might need were not present in certain foods.
Four years later a Polish scientist named Casimir Funk called attention to "a group of indispensable nutritive complexes" in food
stuffs.[37] He called them "vitamines." An editorial in the *Journal of
the American Medical Association* noted in 1918 that a new physiology
of foods was being created that "has emancipated the student of nutrition from the generalities of former days and enabled him to
form more useful conceptions of the specific values of individual
products."[38]

The term "vitamin" was coined in 1921, and the new substances
were given letter names such as Vitamin A and Vitamin B.[39] Information about the importance of vitamins in human diet and their
correlation to disease changed the way in which people thought
about food and meal planning. Fruit was considered an important
source of vitamins and minerals in the new dietary science. An article in the *American Journal of Public Health* in 1927 reported on a
study of bananas in cooperation with United Fruit Company. The
study classed the banana as "an excellent source of vitamins A and
C; a good source of Vitamin B; deficient in Vitamin D and not lack-

ing in Vitamin E." The researchers went on to report that "its potency in C, the availability and the relative cheapness of the fruit, make it a competitor with tomato juice and orange juice for use in infant feeding on vitamin basis alone. Its use will not, however, eliminate the necessity for cod liver oil or sunlight to avoid incidence of rickets."[40]

Readers of the *Ladies Home Journal* learned that "because of the quantity in which bananas may be eaten they are a good source of vitamins. This is why they are classed with other protective foods which have an important place in the diet."[41] In 1930 *Parents Magazine* looked back at a time when "the banana was the forbidden fruit that tempted children. Nowadays doctors frequently advise that boys and girls be given bananas before they have left their cribs. This is another evidence of the progress in nutrition based on scientific discoveries."[42] The American Medical Association approved bananas for advertising in the publications of the Association and for general promulgation to the public in 1931. The Committee on Foods approved the following statement as a basis of claims in the promotion and advertising of bananas:

The banana is available at all seasons. Ripe bananas, or if cooked when partially ripe, are readily digestible even by infants and are valuable for modifying infant milk formulas because of the unique combination of readily assimilable sugars and vitamin C and are an aid against constipation. The vitamin and high carbohydrate content makes the banana a valuable supplement to milk, the mixture being a well balanced food. The carbohydrate contributes materially to the food energy value of mixtures of leafy vegetables and fruits. The final products of metabolism of the banana in the body are alkaline.[43]

In 1935 an analysis of the banana published by United Fruit Company made the claim that the fruit "furnishes fuel, minerals (such as phosphorus, calcium, magnesium, potassium, sodium and iron), and vitamins (A, B, C, and G), at very moderate cost."[44]

The growth in knowledge about public health in the early twentieth century led to public sanitation campaigns, such as street cleaning, and pure food and water supplies. (See Chapter 8 for a more detailed analysis of urban sanitation.) The new science of public health led to dramatic gains in the life expectancy of the people of the United States. Tuberculosis, the greatest killer in history, was a major social problem at the turn of the century as hundreds of thousands of Americans suffered from the disease with a death rate of 201.9 per 100,000 population. The new notions of germs, nutrition, and sanitation combined to provide the weapons in a campaign to eliminate tuberculosis. By 1942 the death rate had dropped to 43.1 per 100,000 and only 7.4 in 1948.[45]

Early symptoms of pulmonary tuberculosis include gradual weight loss, fatigue, and a cough. Before the discovery of antibiotics, the only therapy available was a regimen of fresh air, a nutritious diet, and rest. Most people could not afford to spend a year or more under the treatment of a physician in a sanatorium, and so public health officials searched for ways to prevent and cure the disease while the people who were infected continued to live at home. The tuberculosis movement pioneered many of the methods of public health, including voluntary associations devoted to restricting a specific disease, close cooperation between physicians and the public and between private and public agencies in health work, and campaigns of mass public education.[46]

Undernourished children living in crowded urban districts at great risk of contracting the disease became a prime target of the efforts of tuberculosis associations and other public health agencies. Most children were easy to reach because they attended public schools. Education programs expanded to include school lunch programs and summer camps for the children at greatest risk. Tuberculosis associations also provided medical facilities and services including dispensaries, visiting nurses, camps, classes, open-air schools, "preventoria" for children, and sanatoria for the sick.[47]

In the summer of 1926, a "Sunshine Camp" was organized in Cambridge, Massachusetts, by the Anti-Tuberculosis Association in conjunction with the public schools. The camp served twenty girls

BANANAS
The Body Builder

KEEP BANANAS ON THE PAN-TRY SHELF regularly—the year around. Don't keep them in the ice-box.

Serve them in some fashion—cooked or raw—at all meals. Give them to the kiddies "between times."

Eat them when they are thoroughly ripe —as the golden skin begins to mottle into dark brown. Then the luscious sugary pulp is at its best—delightful to taste, easy to digest, and of rare tissue building quality.

"Yes! Bananas the Body Builder," from *Yes! 100 Ways To Enjoy Bananas* (New Orleans: Bauerlein, 1925), 17.

ages seven to twelve who were considered to be pretubercular "because of their undernourishment and poor habits of life."[48] Camps such as the one in Cambridge offered children an outdoor life with plenty of food, rest, play, and nature study. The children were also taught health habits such as tooth brushing and "no spitting."

The banana was a popular food for combating malnutrition since it was cheap, filling, needed no preparation, and children liked it. The children in Cambridge were given oranges twice a week and received ripe bananas and milk every day as these were considered to "supplement each other exceedingly well in providing essentials for growth."[49] The successful pilot program was followed the next summer by a more ambitious undertaking. Two camps held at the Cambridge public schools, each with four hundred children, offered a morning snack, games, singing, posture work, training in health and food habits, dinner, nap, sewing, basketry, other handiwork, and sandwiches, milk, and bananas before dismissal. Much of the cost of the food was borne by the Anti-Tuberculosis Society.[50] A photograph with the caption "Lunch Hour at the Summer Camp" shows a group of children wearing only shorts, posed by tables holding pitchers of milk while great stalks of bananas hang from the rafters of an outdoor pavilion.[51]

The Bangor, Maine, Anti-Tuberculosis Association also sponsored a summer day camp for underprivileged children "of the pretubercular class." The children received a snack of milk, a banana, and graham crackers every morning.[52] A similar program in Lowell, Massachusetts, provided milk and banana snacks not only for "its adequacy as a supplementary lunch for those children who were in a special need of extra nourishment, but also to create a taste for a palatable food which might replace concentrated carbohydrates in the form of candy, or other sweets, between meals."[53]

A public health survey of the white school children of Iberville Parish in Louisiana in the 1920s indicated that between 47 and 69 percent were underweight, and that their usual diet lacked green vegetables and fruit. As in Cambridge, Massachusetts, bananas and milk were chosen as a dietary supplement. United Fruit donated

"A Good School Lunch" worksheet from 1956, *Bananas for Us,* United Fruit, Education Department (Boston: United Fruit), 4.

twelve bunches of bananas a week for the first three months to get a clinic started. This provided the children with two bananas each as a supplement to their school lunch. Milk was also provided from funds raised by a special benefit. The organizers were pleased to find that children who were not be included in the program—owing to a lack of funds—supplied themselves with bananas and milk at their own expense, in imitation of their friends. This provided a more balanced diet for all the children.[54]

Ninety thousand people died from tuberculosis in the United States in 1930.[55] It wasn't until the 1940s that streptomycin was cultured and found to be effective against the disease.[56] In the meantime, nutrition continued to play an important part in prevention and treatment. In 1939 *Hygeia,* a health magazine published by the American Medical Association, reported on an experiment involving 277 boys and 48,000 bananas. The first group of 123 boys living in an institution were given two or three bananas a day over a period of nine months. The other 154 boys were "denied bananas and used as controls." A guarded report of the results indicated that the children who ate the bananas "may show greater progress in growth than a youngster who is deprived of them."[57] It seems to have been a cruel study for such meager results but perhaps the boys got tired of eating three bananas a day and shared the bananas clandestinely with the control group. The combination of bananas and milk has endured. In 1976 Dole advertised "The 60 Second Breakfast," advising readers that a banana and a glass of milk "satisfied that morning emptiness with delicious natural flavor."[58]

With the identification of vitamins and calories, physicians, research scientists, and dietitians searched for ways in which various foods would not only balance the average person's diet, but also serve as cures for common diseases following the example of citrus fruit and scurvy. *Practical Dietetics for Adults and Children in Health and Disease,* published in 1928, "strongly recommended [bananas] for cases of chronic appendicitis; they should, however, be prohibited in cases of asthma bronchiale."[59] The fruit was promoted as an excellent food for people with kidney trouble as the banana was said to be "deficient in organic salts and it therefore leaves little residue to be eliminated by the kidneys."[60] In addition bananas were recommended as a particularly valuable food for nephritic patients in a 1917 issue of the *Journal of the American Medical Association.*[61]

The Research Department of United Fruit Company was particularly interested in promoting the curative properties of the banana and in 1935 published *Dietary Uses of the Banana in Health and Disease* with the claim that

> in disease, it is suited for some of those conditions in which the maintenance of proper nutrition is especially difficult—such as malnutrition and gastro-intestinal disturbances of infancy and childhood, nephritis and colitis in adults. Strange to say, it is sometimes helpful in both overweight and underweight, or in diarrhea and constipation. It is something of a challenge to explain these empirically observed facts.

The next year, the Research Department published a digest of scientific literature concerning the nutritive and therapeutic values of the banana for "the busy physician as well as the nutritionist and dietitian."[62] This digest cited 292 publications that promoted the use of the banana in the treatment of diseases such as diarrhea, ulcers, colitis, tuberculosis, diabetes, obesity, malnutrition, fertility, celiac disease, scurvy, and gout. Many of the citations also promoted bananas in the diet of healthy infants and children.

Celiac disease was diagnosed and named for the first time in the early 1930s. It is a hereditary chronic intestinal malabsorption disorder now known to be caused by intolerance to gluten. It is a childhood disease that causes retarded growth, serious stomach disorders, weakness, and may result in death.[63] The prevalence of the disease is estimated to be about one in three hundred in southwest Ireland and one in five thousand in North America.[64] In the 1920s and 1930s, it was believed that children with the disease could not tolerate milk, carbohydrates, starches, or sugars.[65]

In 1924 Dr. Sidney Haas advocated a banana cure for children suffering from celiac disease. Bananas were found to be tolerated by the children and the fruit in fresh and powdered form was prescribed as a major component of their diet. It appeared that children actually were cured of the disease after one to three years on the diet.[66] United Fruit claimed that "in celiac disease, banana sugars are almost the only carbohydrates which are well utilized, and the banana diet has curative properties."[67]

When the United States entered World War II, the banana trade was severely disrupted. In August 1942 *Newsweek* reported that U-boat sinkings, conversion of fruit ships to war-materiels carriers, and an overburdened railway system combined to halt the flow of bananas to the grocery store.[68] Parents who, a generation or two earlier, would never have given bananas to their sick or even well infants, panicked when the fruit became hard to find. United Fruit announced that it was giving priority to celiac patients and asked physicians to write or wire the Fruit Dispatch Company for supplies. Villar and Osorio, a New York importing company, advised that a "fairly adequate" supply of banana flour was also available to doctors.[69] *Newsweek* reported that a bunch of bananas was rushed from New York to Montreal by Canadian Colonial Airways to save 22-month-old Margo Bradley's life. Mrs. Valentine Dreschel asked the New York *Journal-American* for help in obtaining bananas for her 21-month-old son John, and Brooklyn police in radio cars searched for hours to find twenty-four bananas which they rushed to the home of 15-month-old Helena Gottlieb.[70]

Other reports that two hundred New York babies were in danger of dying of celiac disease because of the banana shortage prompted a new look at the importance of bananas in infant diets. Experts at Johns Hopkins Hospital in Baltimore recommended the use of other fruits such as strained apples, apricots, and pears in place of bananas.[71] Worried parents were reassured that their children would do fine without bananas, since after all, they themselves had grown up without the fruit.

An article in a postwar 1947 *New York Times Magazine* noted that bananas were "back in pre-war quantities, but so greedy have we become for the soft, yellow tropical fruit that even current shipments are not enough to satisfy us. As a consequence, some communities still complain of shortages."[72]

Research continued in the healing and nutritive properties of common foods. In 1949 scientists announced that bananas apparently produced two antibiotics, one active against fungi and the other, like penicillin and streptomycin, active against bacteria. It was suggested that banana skins, known to be germ-proof wrappers, might owe this property to the antibiotics that the fruit produced during the ripening process.[73]

Ten years later, research scientists at the National Heart Institute in Bethesda, Maryland, identified the amines serotonin and norepinephrine in bananas. Serotonin inhibits gastric secretion and stimulates the smooth muscle in the intestine and elsewhere, while norepinephrine is used as a vasoconstrictor agent that mediates autonomic function in the cardiovascular system. The reported therapeutic uses of bananas in celiac disease, peptic ulcers, and constipation may be due to the presence of these amines in bananas.[74] These findings led to the development of new tests for drugs to treat angina pectoris and high blood pressure.[75]

An article in *Organic Gardening* in 1979 reported that "it has been recently discovered that bananas contain L-tryptophan, a natural amino acid that induces sleep." Combined with milk, which also contains L-tryptophan, bananas might make "a very beneficial bedtime snack for an insomniac."[76] Did the thousands of children in the 1920s and 1930s who were given bananas and milk every day at school and summer camp feel drowsy afterwards?

In 1995 reports were published of a new project, conducted by Charles J. Arntzen at Texas A&M University, to genetically engineer bananas that will protect humans from a variety of diseases. Tobacco plants and potatoes have been found to produce proteins that stimulate protective immune reactions in mice, but unfortunately most people are not interested in chewing tobacco or eating raw potato (cooking kills the protein). If bananas could be induced to offer disease protection, they would be especially suitable research subjects because they are cheap, globally popular, and especially appealing to children, the prime target audience for edible vaccines.[77] Enhanced bananas could take the place of vaccination, eliminating concerns about refrigeration for vaccines as well as for clean needles in poor countries. In 1998 researchers reported that they had immunized people against a disease by having them eat several servings of genetically engineered raw potatoes.[78] And genetically engineered bananas are not far behind. Four-inch-tall transgenic banana plants have been grown, but it will take several years before these grow into trees with fruit.

After World War II, affluence, white-collar sedentary jobs, television, and air conditioning combined to fashion a nation of weight- and health-conscious citizens. Weight-loss dieting spawned a major industry of health foods, diet, and exercise programs. It also produced the nutrition pundit. New health concerns included cholesterol, sodium, potassium, and fiber. Fruit-import companies continued to promote the banana as a healthy food for babies, the elderly, athletes, and dieters of all ages. Where the banana once had been extolled as a food for building up underweight children, it was now also promoted as an aid in weight loss. As early as 1934 bananas and milk were recommended for the treatment of obesity "on the grounds of simplicity, low cost, ready availability, palatability, high satiety value, low salt content and demonstrated effectiveness in securing the desired aim."[79]

Dole ran an advertisement in 1977 with "Waist Not, Want Not" in large letters, picturing three middle-aged women wearing leotards and standing around a scale. The copy suggested that bananas were the perfect diet food: "A medium-size Dole banana contains only about 101 calories, no cholesterol and about as much fat as you'll find in lettuce." Readers were assured that "it's one snack that won't go to your waist."[80] An article on bananas in *Good Housekeeping* in 1982 noted that bananas "are low in sodium, high in potassium, have virtually no fat, are cholesterol-free, and contain important vitamins and minerals too; and their easily digested natural fruit sugars supply quick energy."[81]

In 1993 a full-page advertisement in a Newark, New Jersey, newspaper, sponsored by a major supermarket chain and Chiquita bananas, listed the contents of the "perfect yellow package" as follows: fiber, biotin, calcium, pantothenic acid, folic acid, phosphorus, potassium, selenium, magnesium, vitamins A, B1, B2, B6, C, and E, niacin, zinc, manganese, protein, copper, iron, and 18 amino acids.[82] American housewives were supposed to know that all these things were important in the diet of their family members and to feel good about providing them with "The World's Perfect Food."

Athletes consume bananas because of the potassium that is supposed to help their performance and ease leg cramps. The organizers of the 1995 Marine Corps Marathon in Washington, D.C., provided 8,000 bananas to participants in addition to 80,000 cookies, 520 dozen doughnuts, and 6,100 gallons of lemon-lime Gatorade.[83] An advertisement for banana-flavored Power Bar Athletic Energy Food claimed that it was the "first take-anywhere, ripe-everytime, bruise-free, slow-to-spoil, never-slip-on-the-peel, vitamin-packed, energy-enhancing, moist-and-delicious banana," and offered a free, twelve-page *Guide to Nutrition and Energy*.[84] Bananas have become such a symbol of good health that advertisers include them in blurbs for sports clothes such as the one for a women's cycling tank top with "three pockets in the back [that] can hold a banana, a sandwich or even your pet hamster."[85] The picture of the garment included a banana and a Power Bar.

Bananas hold a secure place in our folklore. Probably more people eat a banana a day than eat the proverbial apple a day to keep the doctor away. Some people claim that their daily banana is the secret of their longevity; others count on it for digestive-tract regularity. In addition bananas have been used to cure corns, warts, headaches, and stage fright. An advertisement in 1918 read "Hooray for Banana Peel 'Gets-It' Only Real Way to Get Rid of Corns."[86] And a 1993 advice column by Ann Landers discussed various methods of wart removal including "the miraculous use of a banana peel."[87] Letters to Ann Landers in 1997 included a treatment for headache with the instructions to

> peel a banana, take half the banana peel and place it on the forehead with the inside of the peel next to the skin. Secure this with a headband or some strip of cloth. Take the other half, place it on the back of the neck and secure it also. Be sure the banana peels are secured very snugly and the white mushy stuff on the inside of the peel is next to the skin. Eighty-five percent of the people who have tried this say they get relief within 30 minutes.[88]

The reader submitting this "cure" noted that his "great-grandfather, Dr. J. B. Frymire, a graduate of the University of Louisville School of Medicine in 1867, started using the banana-peel treatment in the 1890s. "Thousands have written to me to say it works." A second column with letters supporting and deriding the "cure" appeared several months later.[89]

A musician friend confided that she eats a banana before each concert to take the edge off her stage fright. The nutritional and medicinal claims for the banana have shifted over the years, but the perceived connection between the banana and nutrition or disease has remained strong and the popularity of the banana has continued to increase. Advertising departments have taken full advantage of the health-benefit claims for bananas since the early years of the twentieth century and will no doubt continue to do so far into the twenty-first.

6

EATING

Bananas

AT THE BEGINNING OF THE twentieth century, the diet of the average American was transformed by the increasing availability of processed and packaged food, the passage of pure food laws, the expansion of an efficient transportation system, and the growing knowledge of the science of nutrition and sanitation. All this contributed to increasing life expectancy and better health in the United States. Fresh fruit, particularly bananas, were part of the profound alterations to the American diet, to people's images of themselves, to tension between tradition and change, and to the fabric of daily social life. Within a fifty-year period, bananas lost their novelty and luxury status and became a staple item. Bananas disappeared from formal menus and etiquette books and became the comfort food of childhood and old age.

Before the 1880s, bananas were a luxury; expensive, they were served only on important occasions and used in small quantities to display wealth and sophistication. A recipe for banana pudding was included with the menu for a Christening Collation in 1876.[1] A well-known cookbook author noted that as part of the Christmas dinner "fruits—bananas, white grapes, oranges, and late pears—will probably be partaken of sparingly, but must not be omitted."[2]

Another wrote that "a dish of apples, oranges, bananas, and white grapes, placed at one end of the table, and another dish filled with cracked hickory nuts, walnuts, and butternuts, make a pleasant finale to the Christmas dinner."[3] Banana jelly (chopped banana in gelatine) was recommended as a Thanksgiving Day treat.[4]

The menu for the thirty-eighth anniversary dinner given on December 22, 1857, of the New England Society—marking the embarkation of the Pilgrims from Delft Haven—listed apples, oranges, bananas, prunes, figs, raisins, almonds, chestnuts, and walnuts as dessert.[5] Bananas were also included on the menus of fashionable hotels such as the Hotel Ponce de Leon in Saint Augustine, Florida, and Willard's Hotel in Washington, D.C., for both breakfast and dessert. In June 1880 the Glen House in the White Mountains included bananas on the dessert menu with English walnuts, almonds, pecan nuts, raisins, assorted cake, vanilla ice cream, wine jelly, and strawberries with cream.[6] Bananas were also included as part of an elegant dinner in a discussion of "The Perfection of Table Manners" in 1890:

> These are the dishes that, upon her order, were brought for her dinner: Turtle soup, blue fish, roast beef, cold boned capon, fricasseed chicken, lobster salad, stuffed green peppers, boiled new potatoes, stringed beans, New England pudding, a plate of cake, wine jelly, ice cream, an orange, a banana, and a cup of coffee. Each of these being on a separate dish, altogether they occupied considerable space upon the table. She did not eat the whole of any of them, but she did eat freely of all of them. There was no nonsense or fastidiousness about it. She ate what she wanted and as though she wanted it. And yet she did not appear to be eating at all. This is the perfection of table manners. And she knew how to engage in agreeable conversation meantime.[7]

Many Americans turned to etiquette books to find out what to do when confronted with a banana at a formal dinner. It was not con-

sidered polite to pick it up, pull back the skin, and bite off a piece
of the fruit, particularly by women. Fruit was to be eaten with silver
fruit knives and forks.[8] Readers of *The Correct Thing in Good Society*,
published in 1888, were instructed that "it is not the Correct Thing
to eat bananas with the fingers, except at a very informal meal."[9]

Most cookbooks written before 1880 did not include recipes for
bananas. A few recipes appeared in cookbooks published during
the 1880s but the banana was still a luxury item. In 1887 the
Chicago Women's Club published a cookbook with the note that "it
was not the aim of the compilers of this book to furnish a complete
guide to house-keeping, but to collect such rich, rare, and racy, as
well as time-honored, recipes as have never been given to the public."[10] The women included a recipe for Banana Cake in which banana slices were used in the filling rather than in the cake batter.
There were also recipes for Banana Float, in which mashed bananas
were combined with gelatine and milk and served with whipped
cream, and for Graham Mush with Bananas.

The July 23, 1887, issue of *Good Housekeeping* provided a recipe
for

> Heavenly Hash, the newest fashionable dish: oranges, bananas,
> lemons, apples, raisins, and pineapples are cut up into little
> bits, worked just enough to thicken their juices, and then
> served with a little grated nutmeg. But the serving is the pretty
> part. Cut a hole just large enough to admit a spoon in the stem
> end of an orange, and through this hole take out all the inside
> of the orange, which you then fill with the heavenly hash and
> serve on a pretty little glass fruit dish, with lemon or orange
> leaves.[11]

Bananas appeared more frequently as ingredients in cookbook
recipes in the 1890s, but despite their increasing availability, there
were still many books that did not include the fruit. One surprising
omission was from *One Hundred Desserts*, published in 1893, since
most banana recipes were for dessert concoctions.[12] *The American*

Home and Farm Cyclopedia, 1890, had an entry for tropical fruits that included the orange, lemon, lime, banana, and olive, stating that they were "cultivated in the Southern States and California with success, and the interest in their culture is continually increasing."[13] This was the only mention of the banana in the thousand-page work. Some bananas were grown in southern Florida and along the Gulf coast, but there is no other evidence that they were being grown in California in 1890.

The *Encyclopedia of Practical Cookery* noted that "it is certain that Bananas as supplied to us here are a very inferior class of fruit, and of little or no use for dessert, cooking, or any other purpose." Despite this dark assessment of the banana, recipes were provided for baked bananas, banana ice cream, banana cream pie, banana fritters, banana syrup, and a compote of boiled bananas to be served over rice.[14]

By 1900 American cooks were experimenting with bananas in a variety of disguises. Deep-fried banana fritters appeared with some regularity as suggested accompaniments to meat, and banana ice cream was popular. A newspaper article in 1916 explained that bananas could be baked and

> placed on a platter and served as a meat. It is not, however,
> turned out of the skin. When ready to eat it split the skin and
> banana lengthwise of the fruit; season it with salt, pepper, and a
> little butter. In warm weather baked bananas may be used to
> take the place of meat at a meal.[15]

The *American Domestic Cyclopaedia* included recipes for banana cake (slices of fruit between the layers), banana pie, ambrosia (a mixture of pineapple, banana, and coconut), fried bananas, and fruit salad. The fruit salad was described as "a new dish with which epicures tempt fate and give an impetus to stomach anodynes [which] is composed of sliced oranges, sliced pineapples, sliced bananas, sliced hard-boiled eggs, sliced cucumbers, vinegar, and sugar."[16] It is no wonder that some people considered bananas indigestible.

Fruit in a gelatine mold, the forerunner of Jello, was a popular dessert. One recipe for "Fancy Pudding" instructed the cook with a sweet tooth to

> soak 1 box gelatine in 1 pint sherry, add 1 pint boiling water and 1 cup sugar. Put in a mold, and when beginning to stiffen add 2 oranges sliced, 1 banana sliced, a few figs, cut, ¼ pound candied cherries, and if liked, ¼ pound chocolate creams. Serve with whipped cream sweetened and flavored with wine.[17]

Bananas were not always eaten at dinner. They might appear at breakfast "sprinkled with pepper and salt, and served in small, round dishes." Oranges, bananas, and pineapple, "chopped very fine and served with a rich lemonade" and presented in the orange shell, might also be offered to guests for breakfast.[18]

In 1910 an advertisement for Puffed Wheat and Puffed Rice showed a bowl of sliced bananas with a little cereal being spooned over it.[19] Soon it became more common to add sliced bananas to a bowl full of breakfast cereal. A 1918 advertisement for the same cereal included a picture of a bowl of cereal topped with sliced bananas.[20] Ralston advertised a "Morning Appetite Tempter! Crisp, delicious Shredded Ralston topped with sliced bananas and milk or cream. Energy and flavor in every bite. Try it!"[21]

As late as 1921, an article in *Scientific American,* focusing on the digestibility of bananas, advised that mixing a banana "with bread or cereal prevents it from forming a mucilaginous mass in the stomach and thus promotes its digestion, while baking it quickly in the skin until soft and juicy renders it perfectly harmless for most persons."[22] A recipe book published by United's Fruit Dispatch Company in 1924 also promoted the combination of bananas and dry cereal, suggesting

CORN FLAKES WITH BANANAS
Fill a cereal bowl half full of corn flakes, and cut one half of a ripe banana on top of this, and serve with heavy cream, and

sugar if desired (though it will be found that for the average taste the banana supplies the necessary sugar element in a natural form).

NOTE: Grape Nuts, Shredded Wheat, Bran Flakes, etc., may also be served the same way.[23]

Breakfast cereal packaging continues to show the product with sliced banana as a serving suggestion. In the 1980s United Fruit, in cooperation with Nabisco, promoted bananas as a go-together with breakfast cereal, placing stickers on the fruit advertising Nabisco products. In 1986 *Reader's Digest* assumed that Americans ate all their bananas with cereal for breakfast, noting that "sanitation engineers annually haul away more than 13 billion banana peels after we've each plunked 22 pounds of the fruit into our bowls of soggy cereal."[24] This is, indeed, perhaps the most common way in which Americans at the end of the twentieth century consume bananas, despite decades of effort by United Fruit and others to get us to include the fruit in all our meals and between-meal snacks.

A supermarket survey in the Washington, D.C., area in August 1995 found only two kinds of breakfast cereal that paired bananas with the product pictured on the box. One was Health Valley Fiber 7 Flakes and the other was a house brand variety of frosted flakes, neither of them available in other local supermarket chains. Post offered Banana Nut Crunch cereal that was flavored with bananas and Instant Quaker Oatmeal was available with Bananas and Cream flavoring. The most popular fruit displayed with the wide variety of breakfast cereals were strawberries and raspberries. However, Rice Crispy packages sold in Vermont at the same time pictured bananas with the cereal. Cereal companies now offer different packaging to specific regional markets, and depict various fruits with the product depending upon the season and local preferences.

United Fruit published *A Short History of the Banana and a Few Recipes for Its Use* in 1904 with the stated object to teach people to use bananas cooked as a vegetable for lunch and dinner in order to expand the use and consumption of the fruit.[25] For banana entrees

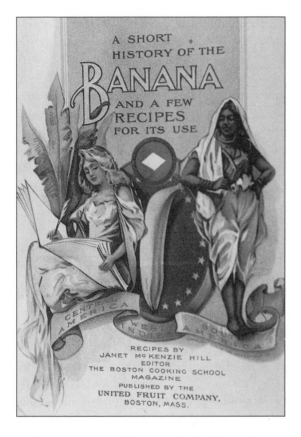

A Short History of the Banana and a Few Recipes for Its Use (Boston: United Fruit, 1904).

the booklet included three recipes for bananas and hot cereal, four baked and two fried banana recipes, hashed lamb and bananas, banana croquettes with lamb chops, compote of bananas with orange syrup, and banana fritters.

As bananas became more common and less expensive at the turn of the century, they began to lose their status as a luxury item. In 1889 bananas were recommended as a substitute for pie in the working man's dinner pail because "if we estimate the ruin wrought upon digestion by pastry and doughnuts, we are ready to affirm that he could better afford hot-house fruits at their dearest, than to satisfy the cravings of nature with these home-made 'delicacies.'"[26]

In 1894 an article in *Harper's Weekly* noted that "if it wasn't for the women and children in this country, the banana trade wouldn't be worth a rap." Women were credited with the sudden enormous growth in the banana trade. According to the article's author, although the dealers preferred red bananas, most of the bananas imported were "of the yellow kind. . . . The women and children like them better."[27] Readers were assured that the "most delicate and nutritious" banana was the great seedless fruit of the world, more of a staple than wheat.

Sidney Mintz suggests that women have traditionally saved the most nutritious food for the men of the family while they and their small children have eaten the scraps.[28] When sugar became widely available and affordable in England, women consumed it in tea and cheap baked goods for quick energy in place of more satisfying but expensive meat. Bananas may have served much the same purpose as sugar for turn-of-the-century American working-class women and children. The fruit was cheap, filling, and nutritious, and soon became known as women and children's food in the United States. In 1892 the author of *A Bill of Fare for Everyday in the Year* suggested that "two or three bananas, sliced in a bowl of bread and milk, make a delicious and sufficient lunch," most likely for women and children.[29] In 1896 a suggested ladies' luncheon menu included bouillon, wafers, banana sandwiches, marshmallow cakes, and tea. According to the contributor, "Banana sandwiches are new and very nice."[30] Not very nutritious by today's standards, but it would have been considered very dainty and feminine and would have provided plenty of quick energy.

As the volume of banana imports continued to increase in the twentieth century, the fruit became an integral part of the American diet in all parts of the country. Bananas were offered to immigrants who came through Ellis Island in New York as their first taste

Yes! 100 Ways to Enjoy Bananas (New Orleans: Bauerlein, 1925).

of America. Even though the fruit itself was imported, European immigrants equated it with the United States and with what real Americans ate.[31]

Good Housekeeping published an article on bananas in 1917 with the observation that "perhaps no staple article of food is more the subject of strange fancies or more misunderstood—more over-praised for qualities which it does not possess and blamed for defects not its own—than that standby of the corner fruit-stand, the banana."[32] The author estimated that seven billion were consumed each year for an average of nearly 72 bananas for each American. This was a tremendous number of bananas. In 1990 the average banana consumption was 52 per capita, still the most widely-eaten fruit in the country.

During World War I, despite the disruption of the banana trade to the United States and the loss of European markets, the possibilities of increased use of bananas were seriously explored in the United States as a substitute for cereal and other carbohydrate food.[33] An article in *Good Housekeeping* notified readers that "your government is urging you to substitute other foods for wheat. Did you know that you can use bananas for this purpose?" The article went on to say that "used in conjunction with dried beans or peas or with dairy products, such as milk and cheese or with lean meat, they serve to secure a properly balanced ration," and included recipes for baked bananas de luxe, banana pickle, banana butter, bananas baked in lemon juice, banana pie, and orange-pecan salad with bananas.[34] According to another article, the banana

is practically the only food which during the last two years has not shown a marked increase in price and to-day will stand comparison with any food upon the market on the basis of caloric costs. Everything points to its continued favor not merely as the "poor man's fruit" as it has sometimes been called, but as a staple food for universal use, and it is to be hoped that it will be employed in continually increasing amounts whether as a substitute for other foods which have become prohibitive in price or because of its own inherent quality.[35]

An article entitled "A Cheap Food We Overlook" in the *Ladies Home Journal* in March 1918 also recommended bananas as a nourishing food. According to the author, bananas have three times the proteid of apples, more fats and a third more carbohydrates. About two pounds and three-quarters of peeled bananas, costing, say, twelve cents, are equal in nutriment to a pound of porterhouse steak. The banana is also rich in mineral salts, containing as much iron as whole-wheat bread and outranking the potato in energy-giving qualities.[36]

Recipes were given for banana croquettes (served hot with any kind of roast meat), banana fritters, baked bananas, banana pudding, banana-and-nut mold, spiced bananas, and fried bananas.

Yet another magazine article, published in 1918 with the title "Cook Your Bananas," stated that

the reason why the banana is not sufficiently appreciated as a food is that we persist in eating it unripe and raw. We might as well eat raw potatoes as to eat bananas in the condition in which they are usually offered. The remedy is to treat them as we do the potato—namely, cook them.[37]

United Fruit Company continued to promote the idea of cooked bananas with a new publication in 1926 that included eighty-three banana recipes. In the entree section suggestions included baked, broiled, and deep-fried bananas, rice and bananas, bananas and poached eggs, banana fritters, and meat loaf with baked bananas and tomato halves. Salad recipes included bananas with other fruit, and bananas in cole slaw. The majority of the recipes were devoted to desserts, ice cream, cakes, and frosting. Under "Special Dishes" are listed banana marmalade recommended to be served with toast, with meat, or as a cake filling, banana muffins, and banana pancakes. These recipes were said to be "absolutely novel and at the same time more delicious in flavor than the old and familiar muffins and marmalade."[38] In 1939 United Fruit claimed that "among the most popular combinations are cooked bananas with meats—roasts, meat loaves, hamburg steak,

Cook Bananas . . . and Win New Hostess Fame! (n.p., c. 1935).

sausages, frankfurters, hash, chops, steaks—or with any fish or fish cakes."[39]

The company has continued through the years to encourage North Americans to cook their bananas and *The Chiquita Banana Cookbook*, published in 1974, included sections on Dips and Drinks, Salads, Vegetables, Barbecue, Entrees, Children's Treats, Baking,

"Bananas and Bacon: Guaranteed to start conversation,"
The New Banana (New York: Fruit Dispatch Company,
United Fruit, 1931).

Desserts, and Flambés and Fondues.[40] The many color illustrations
showed banana preparations such as Banana Plantation Salad,
Tropical Trifle, Spanish Rum Cake, Chicken Honduras, Fish Fillets
Tropical, and Puchero—"the national dish of every Spanish ori-
ented culture"—in tropical, Hispanic settings, clearly not main-

stream United States cuisine. Despite the best efforts of banana promoters, cooked bananas have never taken their place on the average menu. Plantains are favored in Central American and African cuisine, but the cooked banana has never become widely popular on the dinner table in the United States, other than in desserts.

United Fruit also promoted bananas as a between-meal snack, both raw and in combination with ice cream and other soda fountain confections. A soda fountain treat that made a hit in the 1920s and remains popular today is the banana split. Latrobe, Pennsylvania, is credited with creating the first banana split in 1904.[41] Made with a banana cut in half lengthwise, two or three scoops of ice cream, chocolate sauce, strawberry sauce, whipped cream, and a maraschino cherry, it has become a perennial favorite with teenagers. Students at Garringer High School in Charlotte, North Carolina, put together the world's largest banana split in the gym in 1967 using 500 bananas, 45 gallons of ice cream, and 12 gallons of toppings plus an unnamed quantity of whipped cream. It was 250 feet long and fed 300 students.[42]

In 1976 the *Ladies Home Journal* published an article on bananas with the question "Is there anybody anywhere who doesn't know how to make a banana split?" In case there was, the article continued, "the neat thing about that sinfully fattening, wonderfully delicious dish is there is no recipe," instructing readers to assemble bananas, at least three flavors of ice cream, plus an assortment of toppings, whipped cream, chopped nuts, and maraschino cherries and then construct their own.[43] Special oblong banana split dishes are sold to accommodate the sweet and messy treat. Other gooey ice cream and banana combinations are called banana boats or banana barges. Every ice cream store and soda fountain advertises the banana split but it is rare to see a person eat one. With growing adult concern over cholesterol and calories, banana splits are left to the teenagers. Banana splits are still a special concoction, expensive, and only consumed on special occasions, perhaps to share on a date.

Banana bread is said to have been invented by a Depression-era housewife in search of a way to make some extra money at home. It is curious that it took so long to discover, for since the 1930s, banana bread has taken its place on the menu in millions of homes. Grocery stores often provide customers with banana bread recipes when bananas have begun to brown, in a last-ditch attempt to sell their produce. Faced with overripe bananas, many cooks turn them into banana muffins or banana pancakes. Homemade banana bread is considered a thoughtful hostess present, good for breakfast, with a cup of coffee or tea, with lunch or dinner.

In the twenty-first century, as fewer women have the time to bake, banana bread is quick and easy, and it satisfies the urge to bake something fresh. There are even packaged banana bread mixes available for people without the time or inclination to mash their own bananas. Carlene Jolley, a resident of Fulton, Kentucky, and veteran of thirty years of banana-cooking contests, claimed banana bread as her specialty. At Thanksgiving, she filled a wicker turkey with banana muffins and banana breadsticks as a table centerpiece.[44]

Banana pudding has also become an American staple. Made with layers of sliced bananas, vanilla cookies, and vanilla pudding, it is seldom found in fancy restaurants but is a favorite family dessert. For many, it is comfort food—sweet and soft, reminiscent of childhood. It is often found in diners and other restaurants featuring "home cooking." Boxes of Nabisco 'Nilla Wafers and Sunshine Vanilla Wafers picture a dish of banana pudding with slices of fruit and the wafers prominently displayed. The boxes do not carry a recipe for the pudding; everyone is expected to recognize the combination and to be able to recreate it without help. Banana pudding with vanilla cookies embedded in it is a favorite that can also be found in the take-out food section in many supermarkets. It is homey and comfortable and appeals to customers looking for a simple meal.

At the turn of the century, bananas were often referred to as the children's fruit: easy and fun to eat. Parents did not have to worry about seeds or pits. The banana even came with its own holder when the peel was pulled back halfway. Suggested recipes for children's

New Tempting ways to serve bananas (New York: Home Economics Department, Fruit Dispatch Company, 1939).

Chiquita Banana's Recipe Book (New York: Home Economics Department, United Fruit, 1956).

parties often included bananas. An article in a 1911 issue of *American Homes and Gardens* suggested that bananas and other fruit could be arranged to look like pigs, elephants, birds, and tramps. "Let the reader prepare a few such "banana animals" and arrange them upon plates with a little colored paper shaving, and she will be surprised at the wild delight which her handiwork will call forth."[45] Children today enjoy frozen bananas with chocolate coating. The coating kit can be purchased in the supermarket, often displayed in the produce section with the bananas. Other lasting childhood favorites are banana pudding, and peanut butter and banana sandwiches.

The owners of the Elvis Is Alive Museum and Cafe in Wright City,

Missouri, claim that peanut butter and banana sandwiches fried in butter were a favorite of the King. According to one nutritionist, such a sandwich would have 815 calories and 60 grams of fat, equal to the daily total recommended intake of fat for an adult male. Elvis is said also to have enjoyed glazed donuts, cheeseburgers, and frosted brownies. According to registered dietitian Chris Rosenbloom, "the diet might have killed him if other causes didn't."[46]

Despite the short shelf life of raw bananas, the processed banana industry was slow to develop. Once planted in rotation on acreage in Central America, the fruit can be harvested every seven to ten days throughout the year and then sold locally or exported by ship.[47] Temperature control can aid in prolonging the ripening time, but the fruit will inevitably ripen and eventually rot. Since the fruit is available throughout the year, efforts to preserve bananas have not met with much support although attempts have been made to process the fruit in order to include it in the daily diet in new ways.

In the 1886 *Grocers' Handbook* it was explained that bananas could be preserved with sugar and with vinegar, used as bread, and when pressed and fermented would yield "a spirituous drink resembling cider. The sap also makes an excellent wine."[48] United Fruit experimented with various ways to use overripe or scarred bananas that were not fit to be sold on the American market. In 1929 the company announced that laboratory experiments conducted by Harry von Loesecke showed that cider and vinegar could be made from bananas. "Unfortunately, circumstances did not permit the work to be carried beyond laboratory-scale production, but it is hoped the present results may at some time serve as a nucleus for further work on a semi-commercial scale."[49] The idea lay dormant but has not died. A French patent was awarded in 1972 for banana wine and vinegar.[50] Fermented bananas are used in making low-alcohol beer in East Africa and in Central America, but the drink has not achieved popularity in the United States.

Other banana products can be divided into two types: those made from green, starchy bananas, and those made from ripe bananas.

Banana sugar is powdered ripe banana; banana meal is usually made from unripe bananas.[51] Additional processed banana products include banana puree, canned slices, banana figs (dried ripe fingers), banana flour made from dried whole green fruit, banana chips (green slices fried in vegetable oil), and banana essence or extract used as a flavoring. In the Philippines spicy banana catsup is a popular condiment. In addition bananas can be powdered, flaked, freeze-dried, and made into jam and juice.

In 1885 dried bananas were touted in a New York City newspaper as

> among the latest novelties. They are said to be an entirely new food product, and are certainly delicious. The rind of the ripe fruit is removed, and it is dried without sugar, forming dark-colored firm preserve of slightly softer consistency than citron, and having the flavor of a ripe banana. The fruit retains about one-third of its original size, and may be either eaten from the hand, stewed or cooked in cake or pastry. Banana fritters from them are superior to the natural fruit, which comes to this market green and is ripened in hot rooms.[52]

Dried bananas weighed one-ninth of fresh fruit and took up less space so that it was estimated that they would offer large savings in transportation, handling, and storage costs.[53] Dried bananas might be pressed into barrels or boxes, or chopped up fine "with a large sausage-meat cutter" and packed in attractive one-pound paper packages. "In the latter shape, they will make an excellent breakfast food, and can be used for cakes, puddings, ice creams, and numerous other purposes. Also, if heavily compressed in a small space, they will make an ideal ration for soldiers or travelers on long inland tours."[54]

Ten years later, *Scientific American* announced that "dried bananas, or banana figs, as they are called, are now in the market, and will undoubtedly be a great article of trade as soon as found by the schoolboy. They are sweet, wholesome and nourishing."[55] Dried

bananas are available today in health food stores, but they never really caught on, perhaps owing to their unprepossessing brown,
shriveled appearance, or to the development of a commercial
candy industry that caters to the schoolchild's sweet tooth in other
ways.

Other entrepreneurs experimented with banana flour. An article
in *Scientific American* in 1891 suggested that the "hundreds of
thousands of discarded bunches each year" in Jamaica might be
processed into banana flour. The rejected fruit might be under-
sized, undeveloped, or too ripe for American buyers. The author
pointed out that two types of inventions were sorely needed in the
West Indies: a desiccating process and a flour- or meal-making
process. "Wherever one travels in the banana-producing regions,
from Demerara to British Honduras, from Colon to Samana Bay,
the cry will be heard at every large plantation, 'Oh! if someone
would only invent and perfect a drying or preserving process that
could be depended on.'"[56]

Part of the problem was discrimination by the wholesalers and
railroads against small bunches. In the 1890s railroads charged by
the bunch instead of by weight, making it more cost effective for
companies to deal with large bunches. An article in *Scientific American* complained that "to the man who buys a nickel's worth of bananas it ought to be immaterial whether they come off a six hands
bunch or a ten hands."[57]

The invention of the steamship and refrigeration, as well as the
expansion of the American market, helped to reduce some of the
waste in the banana-growing industry. Articles in *Scientific American*
in 1899 and 1900 continued to promote the notion of dried banana
flour based on the new ideas of nutrition rather than availability.
The first noted that banana flour had the potential to "prove to be
the basis of a very valuable industry," and went on to explain that
"since flour can be produced from [bananas] at less expense than
that obtained from wheat, it is permissible to believe that the products of the banana plant will furnish the working classes of many
countries with wholesome, nourishing food at the lowest possible

cost."[58] The author admitted that "the flavor of the dry banana is somewhat strange at first, but the palate soon adapts itself to the taste." An article the next year noted that the banana

> is very nutritive, and forms a nearly perfect food. It contains more than 25 percent of assimilable organic matter. According to Humbolt, it is forty-eight times more nutritious than the potato, while Crichton Campbell has stated that the banana is twenty-five times more nutritious than the best wheaten bread.[59]

In Venezuela it was said that banana flour was fed to children, aged people, convalescents, nursing women, and "is of great service in the feeding of those suffering from complaints of the stomach." Banana flour "may be used in the same way as wheaten flour, except for the preparation of bread, for which it is unsuitable, inasmuch as it contains no gluten."[60]

During World War I, entrepreneurs in Jamaica suggested that banana flour would make an excellent substitute for wheat and rye flour, arguing that it would cost less than wheat flour and "has a nutritive value equal, if not superior, to any cereal flour."[61] It was proposed that banana meal could be mixed with wheat flour and made into bread and cake, particularly ginger bread and ginger cakes, and that scones could be made entirely from banana meal in place of wheat flour. Americans were assured that "the high sugar content makes the banana flour much more palatable and certainly more nutritious than the plain starch flour produced by the German government from potatoes and used as a war bread."[62]

The U.S. Department of Agriculture with the cooperation of United Fruit experimented with the manufacture of banana flour and announced in 1917 that, with the proper facilities at Caribbean seaports, "it should be entirely feasible to manufacture into flour an enormous quantity of bananas that are ordinarily too ripe or otherwise unfit for shipment to the United States."[63] However, when the war ended in 1918, the nation forgot the high price of bread, and commercial banana flour processing facilities were never built. This may have been partly due to pressure on the federal government from American wheat growers who had expanded production during the war and were not interested in competition from imported banana flour.

In 1922 improvements in banana-drying technology promoted a revival of interest in dried bananas in the United States.[64] Dried banana chips, made from large bananas rich in starch (plantains?), could be ground into a fine flour and used by biscuit manufacturers to "produce through it a highly palatable, fine flavored, aromatic baked product. It is also used for the baking of cakes, pies, and for confectionery."[65] Proponents of the new industry suggested that "in some ways the properly dehydrated banana is to be preferred to the freshly picked fruit. The food value cost is considerably lower than that of fresh bananas."[66]

Another reason put forward for dried bananas was that only the two or three varieties that traveled well ever appeared in North American ports. A drying process would make a wide variety of bananas available to northern consumers.[67] However, as delicious as they may have been, dried bananas never caught the imagination of the American public nor did they become a culinary staple in the United States. This may be because fresh bananas were widely available at low prices and there was no need for preserving bananas so that they would be available throughout the year.

United Fruit continued to experiment with new banana products that would use otherwise discarded bananas. Company laboratories invented a banana powder, called Melzo, that was approved by the American Medical Association as baby food, combating "an ancient prejudice against the fruit."[68] In 1933 Melzo, produced by the Chase Williams Corporation of New York, was introduced to the American public as a home and soda fountain drink. It contained the new banana powder, along with maltose-dextrin, skimmed milk, yeast, vitamin D, and vanilla.[69] Melzo was marketed as a health food for children and the elderly, as an aid to indigestion, and "as a revitalizer for all who are sluggish mentally or physically."[70] It was ad-

*Yes, We have bananas and in powdered
form* (New York: Nulco Meloban,
The Nulomoline Company, 2d ed.,
1936).

vertised in newspapers and through soda fountain promotions.
Free samples were distributed to soda fountains and $100 cash
prizes were offered "to induce soda jerkers to work out alluring
combinations and actively to sell the public."[71]

World War II again renewed interest in dried or processed bananas to permit "preservation and storage of the fruit during periods when banana stems cannot be shipped."[72] But bananas continued to be eaten fresh or in confectionery such as pies, cakes, and ice cream, when they could be had, with "some consumption, insignificant in volume, of dried bananas for medicinal purposes."[73]

Part of the reason for the experimentation with dried banana products was that peeled fresh bananas within half an hour soften and turn brown, becoming unpalatable. Nutritionists in schools, hospitals, and cafeterias struggled with the problem of how to use the popular, nutritious, and economical fruit since banana dishes enjoyed at home were difficult to serve in institutional settings. In the 1930s experiments were made using cream of tartar and a glucose solution with pineapple and grapefruit juices to coat sliced bananas in order to preserve their color and firmness.[74] This was a reasonably successful solution but added expense and preparation time.

Although Americans seldom cook bananas or serve them with meat, the fruit import companies have managed to expand consumption in other ways. Most processed bananas are used in the manufacture of commercial food products rather than in the home. United Fruit built a modern factory to produce banana puree in Honduras in 1966.[75] Initial demand for this product was low, and only 15,000 tons of Cavendish bananas were processed out of a total of 6.5 million tons exported in 1972.[76] The volume increased considerably in the 1980s with Honduras alone exporting about eight thousand tons of banana puree and one thousand tons of canned banana slices in 1983.

United Brands developed the first commercial, all-natural banana extract that appeared on the market in 1982. Some 3,200 ripe bananas are needed to produce a 3.8 liter bottle of clear, colorless liquid that smells like banana. Banana extract is used in desserts, toppings, juices, and drinks.[77] In 1991 bananas were available in twenty-seven different forms and researchers were working to develop yet more to supply "that little extra flavor, specific product textural qualities, and ease of handling ingredients in the processing plant."[78]

Today banana puree is used to flavor sherbet, ice cream, eggnog, yogurt, and cottage cheese. It is a popular ingredient in banana bread, cake, tarts, muffins, doughnuts, icing, and banana cream pie. Banana puree is also found in a wide variety of baby food products. Gerber and Heinz baby foods include mashed bananas; bananas with tapioca; bananas and strawberries, or bananas and pineapple with tapioca; mixed fruit dessert; banana apple dessert; mixed cereal, oatmeal, or rice cereal with applesauce and bananas; mixed fruit juice; banana pudding; apple banana juice; banana juice medley with low fat yogurt; and banana cookies. In a letter in the newspaper advice column "Hints from Heloise," a reader from Struthers, Ohio, suggested that when making banana bread or cake, two small jars of baby food equal one cup of mashed bananas. "Baby food is easy to store and is always handy."[79]

Banana powder is used in dry mixes and crunch toppings, and banana extract is used to flavor beverages, dairy products, and bakery products.[80] Chiquita and Dole both came out in the 1990s with tropical fruit juice mixtures that include banana. Canned sliced bananas are used mainly in bakery products, desserts, fruit cocktails, fruit salads, and ice cream toppings.[81] In addition, methods to produce frozen, whole, peeled, and sliced bananas have been developed for use in dairy products, frozen novelties, puddings, and bakery products.

Bananas appear in a variety of forms in the supermarket but it is somewhat surprising that banana flavoring is mostly limited to yogurt, baby food, and gelatin desserts. A few cake and banana bread mixes and banana-flavored cereals are available. Chiquita marketed banana-shaped cookies with chocolate bottoms in 1995 but they did not survive the competition with other cookie products in the supermarket. The only banana-flavored cookies in a recent visit to two major grocery chains were found in the baby food section. Ben and Jerry Ice Cream comes in Chunky Monkey: banana flavored with chocolate and nuts—but that, along with strawberry banana frozen yogurt and Friendly's Royal Banana Split Sundae Ice Cream, are the sole banana-flavored frozen desserts in two major chains in the Washington, D.C., area.

Banana or plantain chips are included in some of the snack of-
ferings of grocery stores, and natural food companies that market
dried fruit and nut mixtures are beginning to include bananas.
Planters, a more mainstream company, came out with Caribbean
Crunch Snack Mix that includes peanuts, cashews, sesame snack
sticks, and banana and pineapple pieces.

Bananas may also appear in commercial products as "a flavor
background builder or bodying agent."[82] The fruit softens the
sometimes harsh taste of citric acid while at the same time the flavor does not overpower other ingredients. Bananas are also used as
a thickening agent, adding body and water stabilization to sauces.
Bananas have become an unnoticed ingredient in a number of food
products such as barbecue and other sauces, glazes, gravy, soups,
and salad dressings. Banana-flavored or banana-enhanced products
can now be found throughout the supermarket, not just in the produce aisle.

The United States was known as a nation of fruit eaters in the
nineteenth century. Was the insertion of bananas into the American diet irreversible? Would Americans give up eating bananas if
the price rose in comparison to other fruit? Bananas are so taken
for granted today that it is difficult to imagine consumer protests of
the type that emerged during the tariff controversy in 1924. Would
the millions of people who eat a banana a day quietly switch to another fruit or would they panic the way parents did during the banana shortages of World War II? Bananas are part of our diet and
many people rely on them for health reasons, but they have never
become necessary for a particular holiday celebration the way that
cranberries have. Efforts to pair bananas with meat loaf or hotdogs
were not successful in the way apples complement pork. Bananas
no longer appear at formal meals or on special occasions. Despite
our enormous per capita consumption, the fruit has remained the
"children's food," a snack seldom taken seriously, yet comfortable
and homey.

7

CELEBRATING

Bananas

FOR MANY YEARS, THE TWIN cities of Fulton, Kentucky, and South Fulton, Tennessee, called themselves the Banana Capital of the United States. For a thirty-year period they celebrated with a week-long International Banana Festival that culminated in a parade featuring a one-ton banana pudding. Fulton was the site of a major railroad junction with an ice factory where thousands of railroad cars of bananas were checked before being dispatched throughout the United States. The people of Fulton took something like a banana seriously and made it important. The Fulton banana festival is an example of how the banana has been absorbed into the culture of the United States, adopted by a small Midwestern town and made the focus of community identity.

The residents of Fulton and the peoples of Central America were able to connect with one another through the banana trade, not just by politics and economics but through cultural interests. The initial connection was economic but the festival founders were able to foster it on concerns about communism in Latin America, and a perceived need to bring culture to the children of Fulton.

Today Fulton, Kentucky, is a quiet agricultural town near the Mississippi River of just over three thousand residents, surrounded by

Downtown Fulton, Kentucky, during the Thirtieth Annual International Banana Festival (September 1992).

corn and tobacco fields. The largest structure in town is the grain elevator. South Fulton, Tennessee, just across the state line, has a population of just under three thousand. But Fulton was not always so quiet. The Illinois Central Railroad, the first to develop refrigerated cars, began shipping bananas out of New Orleans in 1880.[1] Freight trains of the Illinois Central Gulf Railroad with a hundred or more cars loaded with bananas regularly traveled the line north from New Orleans to Fulton, one of the major intersections in the national railway system where five lines met. Here they were serviced and separated to be assigned to trains traveling north, east, and west. More than half the bananas imported into the United States traveled through Fulton. This explains their claim to being the Banana Capital of the United States.[2]

Their feeling of connectedness to the peoples of Latin America developed through the bananas on the freight trains, even though most of the people in Fulton would never see the banana plantations in the Caribbean tropics or even the actual bananas that passed through their town. They saw just the freight cars being iced in the summer or heated in the winter. Only resident fruit company inspectors opened the boxcar doors and actually touched the fruit. But the connection was there and was actively encouraged during the 1960s and 1970s.

The freight yards were a major employer in Fulton and representatives of the major banana-importing companies, United Fruit and Standard Fruit, lived there. Their job was to inspect the banana cars, checking temperature and making adjustments, to keep the fruit from ripening too quickly in the warm months or from freezing in the winter. Inspectors checked the temperature of the fruit by inserting a thermometer, "like a baby thermometer," into two bananas from each car, top and bottom. One long-time Fulton resident recalled picking up and taking home the bananas in the railroad yard that had been discarded after testing. Inspectors kept records for each car, forwarding them to the company, and kept in touch with service representatives further along the routes to determine what sort of weather the fruit cars might encounter before reaching their various destinations. "Messengers" rode with the fruit trains in the caboose. They were paid expenses and mileage plus $4.00 a day. Eight to ten men would leave New Orleans and accompany the freight as the cars were split off into separate trains in Memphis, Fulton, Blueford, Chicago, Dubuque, Minneapolis, and Cincinnati.

Bill Jolley, a retired inspector of twenty years for Standard Fruit, remembers that it was a worrisome job. If bananas were kept too cold, they would turn black and would not ripen. If they were too hot, they ripened too fast. Company service inspectors wore long rubber gloves to guard against tarantulas when they reached into the banana bunches. Paul Westpheling, long-time publisher of the Fulton newspaper, remembered a friend entering his office one day displaying a small python wrapped around his arm. The snake had been found in a bunch of bananas in one of the freight cars.

At times as many as three or four banana boats a week arrived in

New Orleans and were unloaded onto freight trains. As soon as a train was made up, it started on its way. The trip to Fulton took twelve hours. The banana trains often arrived in clusters; there might not be any trains for a week or two and then for a couple of days they would come in every three or four hours.[3] The trains might arrive at any time of the day or night, and when the whistle blew, men and boys left their beds, their school books, or their regular jobs to head for the freight yards to service the arriving train.

One resident remembered that boys first got a paper route, then as they got older went to work icing railroad cars. The young workers were known as banana monkeys. Bill Robertson, Fulton City commissioner and retired teacher, remembers getting calls at the high school for twenty-five boys to ice a banana train. When the banana trains came in at night, the boys would be sleepy the next day in class. It was considered a good job because servicing often only took only one or two hours with workers paid for a minimum of four hours.

The Wright ice factory, the largest one-story ice plant in the United States, was founded in 1898 to serve all northbound Illinois Central freight cars.[4] The plant was located at the railroad yard and produced 300-pound blocks of ice for cooling the cars. The blocks were moved by chain along a big frame half a mile long at the same height as the cars. There were tracks on each side of the frame so that cars could be iced from both sides. Men and boys used big metal hooks to move the blocks and then broke them up with picks into 100-pound chunks to be placed in bunkers at each end of a banana car. Each car could take between 600 and 1000 pounds.

In the winter heaters were placed in the compartments instead of ice. At first the heaters used charcoal; later they used alcohol or kerosene. Eventually heaters had thermostats which made them easier to control. The freight cars also had vents which the inspectors could adjust by guesstimate to control the temperature. As they were serviced, switch engines moved the freight cars around the railroad yard and reorganized them into smaller trains for further destinations.

The germ of the idea for the International Banana Festival came when Johanna Westpheling, editor of the local Fulton paper, accompanied a Fulton high school singer and ukulele player to the Arthur Godfrey show in 1958. As Mrs. Westpheling was talking with Godfrey, she described Fulton as the Banana Capital of the United States, which caught his attention. According to the Memphis *Commercial Appeal,* "the girl was good. Godfrey kept inviting her back, and Mrs. Westpheling kept coming with her, plugging Fulton bananas each chance she got."[5]

Mrs. Westpheling had been a reporter for the *Washington Post* and the *Washington Star* during World War II. In 1947 she and her husband, Paul, moved to Fulton where they purchased the *Fulton County News;* Paul was the publisher and Jo the editor. In 1955 they bought the local radio station, which Johanna Westpheling managed. Paul Westpheling eventually became the president of the Ken-Tenn Broadcasting Corporation. To this they added the *Fulton Shopper* weekly newspaper in 1966.[6]

Back home in Fulton, Mrs. Westpheling and a group of friends were "sitting around thinking" of how to promote business and culture in Fulton (which they considered the "cultural desert of America") when the idea of a banana festival began to take shape.[7] According to Nathan Wade, "We kicked the idea around, but it wasn't until five years later we did it."[8] This small group of influential citizens—including Doug Burnett of the Pure Milk Company, Nathan Wade, owner of the furniture factory, and Mary Nelle Wright, wife of the local pharmacist and writer for the paper—appealed for support from the banana companies. Four of the organizers traveled to New Orleans in September 1963 where they met with representatives from the National Association of Banana Agents, a trade group who agreed to match $15,000 in local fund-raising.[9] Gene Bond of the Standard Fruit Company agreed to donate a railroad carload of bananas and to supply financial help for the first festival.[10] (One resident recalled that United Fruit Company would have nothing to do with the festival.)

Over the years Standard Fruit and Dole donated tons of bananas,

some of which went into making enormous annual banana puddings. In 1971 a photograph in the *Fulton County News* showed
"Gene Bond of Standard Fruit and Steamship Company, an ardent
supporter and financial backer of the International Banana Festival from the first year" with the 1971 Banana Festival Princess.[11]
Bunches of bananas were hung on trees, light posts, and parking
meters along the parade route so that spectators might help themselves. There was great indignation when anyone ventured to appropriate an entire stalk.

The group also approached the recently organized Tennessee
and Kentucky Arts Commissions for help with the festival. Over the
years the commissions provided art exhibitions, craft demonstrations and exhibits, classical and jazz concerts, and on one memo-
rable occasion, a traveling troupe from the Joffrey Ballet who performed in a tent. Patricia Alvestia, prima ballerina of Ecuador,
attended the festival in 1967. Not everyone appreciated the program, however. One of the festival organizers remembered one
man complaining about men in leotards.

Jo Westpheling and Mary Nelle Wright also went to Washington
to ask their congressmen for help. They met President John F.
Kennedy and his brother, Robert, who helped organize a sister city
connection with Quito, Ecuador. They were able, as two western
Kentucky women journalists, to travel with Lady Bird Johnson and
enlist her support for the festival, as well as that of the Office of Inter-American Programs, Bureau of Educational and Cultural Affairs
in Washington, D.C., whose deputy director, J. Manuel Espinosa, attended the festival in 1967.[12]

The first festival was held November 4–9, 1963. "With a rail car
full of bananas, a commitment from Miss America, and $3,000, the
first festival took off with an air of blistering excitement."[13] The festival included the Banana Princess Pageant, an appearance by Miss
America 1963, and a one-ton banana pudding. Music was provided
by La Reina Del Ejercito, the Guatemalan Army Marimba Band.[14]
"After it was over, the newly formed festival association, which was
made up of interested citizens, came out proud and with a profit

of more than $20,000," setting in motion plans for an annual festival.[15]

The festival began in the Cold War era of the early 1960s "as an experiment in human relations showing the coincidence of interests between the peoples of the two American continents. . . . The theme, Project-Unite Us, was conceived with the ultimate goal to 'fight communism with bananas.'"[16] According to the program published for the sixth annual festival in 1968, "in their efforts in the field of people-to-people diplomacy Twin Citizens feel that their AMIGO program of friendly understanding between the youth of the two countries is a blow aimed at the beachhead which communism is attempting to establish in these banana-producing countries."[17] The program also contained a statement from the government of the City of Fulton supporting the festival "because we feel that this small gesture, by a small community in Kentucky, has done much more than millions spent through Washington."[18]

Fulton's efforts were very much in the tradition of the American missionary spirit. Americans had long believed that if only other people could be exposed to American culture, they would naturally become like Americans themselves. All one had to do was show visitors American institutions and expose them to American goodwill and all would be well. For example, European middle managers were brought to America after World War II for goodwill tours of factories and businesses combined with barbecues and small-town welcomes under the United States Technical Assistance and Productivity Program, part of the Marshall Plan. One town in Iowa even produced a play for their visitors.[19] It was soon realized that more was needed, however, and large numbers of European middle managers began to attend MBA programs at universities in the United States. Yet the initial impulse was friendship and hospitality.

In the 1960s the banana festival was seen as a truly international affair, bringing together the people of banana-producing countries such as Guatemala, Ecuador, El Salvador, Honduras, Costa Rica, Peru, Colombia, Panama, Nicaragua, Mexico, Argentina, and Venezuela with the people of Middle America through "Project-Unite Us."[20] President Kennedy sent a message to the festival commending the Twin Cities "for contributions to the banana industry, and as a part of vital economic link with our neighbors to the South."[21] President Johnson praised the celebration for its key role in the relations between the United States and Latin America, and in 1967 sent Averill Harriman, undersecretary of state for political affairs, as his personal representative.[22] In addition to Harriman, attendees in 1967 included Ambassadors Jose Antonio Correa of Ecuador and Gonzalo J. Facio of Costa Rica.[23]

Standard Fruit Company sponsored the back page advertisement of the 1970 festival program, congratulating Fulton on its achievement:

THIS FESTIVAL IS AN EXAMPLE OF WHAT A COMMUNITY CAN DO WHEN EVERYONE WORKS TOGETHER TO PROMOTE GOODWILL AND FRIENDSHIP. This festival is, however, much more than a week of local, fun-filled activities. Over the years it has grown into a meaningful goodwill program between the Americas. [It is] a people-to-people project with our neighbors to the south. Today it makes a valuable contribution to inter-American relations. We at Standard Fruit are happy to have been of assistance in developing the first festival in 1962. We enjoy participating each year and look forward to a continuation of successful festivals for years to come.

The idea of the banana festival "hit the fancy of the whole country" as one Fulton resident put it. It was unique and was immediately successful. The early festivals were covered by the Voice of America, and television coverage brought Fulton to national attention. The State Department made several films at the festivals to show in Latin American countries. During the 1960s representatives from banana-producing countries in Latin America who attended the festival included students, diplomats, artists, musicians, reporters, and educators. It was "a real party time for the whole town."[24]

Fulton families hosted twenty-five to fifty Latin American students, ages 16 to 20, for two to three weeks each summer before the festival. The exchange was organized through the Alliance for

Progress and lasted into the late 1970s.[25] It was hoped that the visitors "might see and believe in the kind of people who inhabit a small but typical town in the United States."[26] The students visited schools and churches, went to parties and meetings, and toured the surrounding countryside, businesses, clubs, and community centers. It was hoped that "Fulton's genuine friendliness had done more to enhance understand[ing] and goodwill than a hundred textbooks and a thousand lectures could provide."[27]

As many of the young guests spoke little or no English, the community was provided with Spanish lessons on the local radio station, in the local newspapers, and in the festival programs. In 1968 a Guatemalan student attending Murray State University taught a series of evening classes. Teachers from the Spanish Department of the Louisville, Kentucky, school system attended the festival in 1967 to practice their Spanish.[28] The Fulton public school system, however, did not add Spanish to the curriculum, despite supporting editorials in the local paper.[29]

One of the highlights of the festival in the 1960s was the daily performances of the twelve- to fourteen-member Guatemalan Army Marimba Band. Fulton residents have fond memories of band members playing long into the night in local restaurants and for street dances. The 1968 festival program billed the band as the "stars," the "show stealers," and the "music men," and noted that "their Latin American rhythms fill the air with an irresistible beat that has come to be an integral part of each festival."[30] The band was still attending the festival in 1978. In 1976 the festival program noted that

it is the time to enjoy the beautiful music of the marimba. The members of the Guatemalan Army Marimba Band have become honorary citizens of the twin-cities. They share the same enthusiasm in being re-united with friends.[31]

One resident remembered that the band members were notorious for "missing" their plane connection in New Orleans, necessitating an overnight stay in the city of jazz.

In addition to street dances for adults and teens, festivals might include Latin American dance demonstrations, ballet, and square dance performances. In the early years, a large, four-pole tent in Kitty League Park was the stage for Inter-American programs featuring classical guitarists, folk dancers from Latin America, the Berea College Country Dancers from Kentucky, and country and western shows with stars such as Merle Travis, jazz performer Lionel Hampton and his Band of the Presidents, as well as rock groups such as the Strawberry Alarm Clock. The Cremona Strings, a youth orchestra from "many of the Nashville public and private schools, colleges, and universities," performed in 1970 as did the Junior Company of the Joffery Ballet–Joffrey's II Company.[32]

Festival organizers were also interested in bringing the visual arts to Fulton. Both fine arts and crafts were represented with Latin American basket weavers demonstrating hat and basket making, and a Mayan Indian from Guatemala displaying loom weaving. A Kentucky weaver also displayed her work. Paintings by South American artists were shown and the Kentucky Art Guild Train made a stop in Fulton with displays of Kentucky crafts, drawings, and paintings. The Smithsonian Institution sent an exhibition of Peruvian embroideries created by children ages six to sixteen that, according to the Eighth Festival Program, depicted scenes in a remote village in the Peruvian Andes. Funds raised from the embroideries "are helping to provide their village with books, shoes, and building funds."[33] A U.S. Marine Corps Art Exhibit featured fifty pieces of "combat art" from Vietnam, the "first time this exceptional collection of paintings has been released other than to galleries and the first showing in this area."[34]

The idea for a one-ton banana pudding originated with W. P. "Dub" Burnett, owner of the Pure Milk Company, which later became Turner Dairies. Mr. Burnett "took pride in preparing the famous 1-ton pudding each year" and for many years, the Pure Milk Company of Fulton supplied the 950 pounds of boiled custard for the pudding.[35] However, around 1990, insurance officials deemed this too risky, and packaged pudding had to be substituted for fresh. The 1992 recipe called for "5,000 Dole Bananas, 250 pounds Nabisco Vanilla Wafers, and 950 pounds of Regency Banana Creme Pudding Mix" to serve about 10,000 people.[36]

The pudding was constructed the day before the parade in a room in City Hall. Here volunteers, wearing rubber gloves donated by the local funeral home, peeled the bananas and pushed them through a slicer strung with a number of wires about one-half inch apart. When all the fruit was ready, the pudding was made by layering the ingredients in a large stainless steel container about the size of a bathtub. The original container was made of clear plastic or glass so that the pudding, with its layers of sliced bananas and vanilla wafers, could be seen by parade goers. When that container broke, it was replaced with a steel tub. The completed pudding was stored overnight in a refrigerated truck parked next to City Hall.

The day of the parade, the pudding was maneuvered onto a decorated float with a fork lift. Fulton was proud of holding the record for having the world's largest banana pudding. In 1987, Fultonians constructed a two-ton pudding to celebrate the 25th anniversary of the festival, in a container supplied by the Modern Welding Company. The two-ton pudding was "publicized nationwide, on television, and in countless newspapers and magazines."[37] Festival organizers returned to the one-ton version in later years.

Sports events during the festival varied from year to year. At one festival, the first Inter-American soccer exhibition was held with teams from Costa Rica and Honduras competing. Sports fans also watched an exhibition match by Kentucky golfer and PGA champion Bobby Nichols at the Fulton Country Club.[38] A railroad handcar race was staged another year to commemorate the history of railroading in Fulton.[39] In 1976 the theme was pioneer sporting events that included tobacco spitting, frog jumping, horseshoe pitching, and sack racing.[40] The festival also included the annual football game between the rival high schools of Fulton, Kentucky, and South Fulton, Tennessee.

Each year a beauty pageant was held to select the International Banana Princess who rode on the parade float with the pudding.

Miss America of 1963 and Miss America of 1964 crowned the International Banana Princess for two consecutive years, rode on a special "Miss America" float in the parade, and attended the Miss America Homefolks' Luncheon.[41] At the festival's peak in the late 1960s, young women "from all over the United States" competed for the honor.[42] The winner received a $1,000 college scholarship and a ten-day all-expense paid trip with chaperon to Central America. The four runners-up also received scholarship money. The scholarships were provided for five years by the Price Foundation of Ormond Beach, Florida.[43] In 1969 the princess and her chaperon toured Ecuador for twelve days. The trip was sponsored by Ecuadoriana Air Lines, the Hotel Quito, and the International Banana Festival.[44] In some years there was a Junior Banana Princess and a little Miss and Mr. Banana contest, and beauty queens such as Miss Kentucky, Miss Tennessee, Miss Ecuador, Miss Nicaragua, and the International Dairy Princess participated in the parade.[45]

The festival inspired a number of cooks over the years to think of new ways to incorporate bananas into their recipes. A banana pancake breakfast was held one year, and annual banana bake-off contests were popular. Winning entries included banana cream puffs with caramel topping and custard filling, banana-buttermilk pound cake, a banana cake with cream cheese icing, banana cream pie, banana French coconut pie, banana crunch pie, and peanut butter banana pie. (There were no baked bananas with meat loaf.) The festival inspired several cookbooks including *Go Bananas* with eighty recipes, published in 1992 by "Alana Banana."

During the 1960s the citizens of Fulton went beyond the festival itself to forge links with Latin America. In April 1966 the sister city of Quito, Ecuador, received a visit from a group of thirty Fultonians who "met a range of people there that included the country's president and banana harvesters."[46] They also toured other Central American countries meeting with students who had been guests during the festivals. In 1968 Mrs. Westpheling and Mrs. Wright organized a baby blanket collection for the Rimmer Memorial Hospital in Quito after learning that many infants were discharged wrapped in newspaper. Mrs. Westpheling and Mrs. Wright accompanied a truckload of donated blankets to New Orleans where they were met by the Ecuadorean Counsel General and Mayor Victor C. Schiro, who made the ladies honorary citizens of New Orleans, complete with a certificate. The blankets were shipped to Ecuador by banana boat.

The festival began to decline in the 1970s. In addition to the demise of the railroad banana-freight business, the festival organizers ran into problems with jealousy and local politics. A 1971 urban renewal project tore down the railroad station that had been earmarked for the Art Guild museum and replaced it with public housing. Alternative plans for a Latin-American Friendship Center were frustrated.[47] An editorial written by Jo Westphaling complained that "too few people are willing to endure the hardships of making the dream come true, and too many people simply say 'it wouldn't do Fulton any good' as there are still a couple of sore heads who say the Festival is a waste of time."[48] Hopes for culture for Fulton were frustrated by those who opposed male ballet dancers and preferred country and western to classical music. At the Twenty-fifth Festival, one of the featured attractions was the Chicago Knockers, an "all-girl" mud wrestling team. Festival visitors were invited to watch "eight gorgeous girls—in their repertoire of modeling, dancing, and mud wrestling."[49]

The sense of connection had begun to dwindle in the 1970s when banana trains no longer stopped in Fulton. Fears and concerns about illegal immigration and drug traffic from Latin America made it harder and harder to connect with people a thousand miles away. By 1984, suspicion of Latin Americans took the place of the AMIGO program. The students had become "too much trouble." One of the organizers admitted that she "sold out" in frustration and traveled for ten years, rather than witness what was happening to her creation.[50] She felt that the festival had become a straight carnival without the culture that the original organizers had tried so hard to provide for the citizens of Fulton. She blamed the decline of interest in the festival on younger people who no longer joined civic clubs and who took less interest in the community. Instead of getting involved in local projects, they played golf and tennis and took vacations away from Fulton.

In 1992, very few outside visitors attended the week-long thirtieth annual festival, which included arts and crafts exhibits, a banana bake-off, a football game between the rival high schools, a banana olympics, foot races, an Academic Bowl, decorated shop windows, a carnival, banana derby, talent competition, children's parade, BB shoot and pistol shoot sponsored by the police department, beauty pageants, and church services. The beard contest, tricycle contest, wheelchair race, and shopping-cart race, sponsored by the local hospital, were rained out. A banana-split-eating contest at the Dairy Queen in South Fulton was attended by about fifty people with fewer than a dozen adult and child contestants. Even a new event, the Banana Chip contest, did not draw much attention even though the festival program stated that "this should prove to be a very fun-

Banana license plate, photo taken at Thirtieth Annual International Banana Festival, Fulton, Kentucky (September 1992).

filled event with much suspense." In this contest, Miss Puddin', a cow, was allowed to roam a numbered grid of one-foot squares "until Mother Nature pays her a visit." Each square could be purchased for five dollars. Prize money was paid out depending upon on where the animal dropping landed.[51] It is no wonder that the surviving founders of the festival were no longer interested in attending. Mary Nelle Wright wistfully remarked that the festival had become straight carnival with no culture. The dream of four or five people had blossomed for several years and then faded away. "We tried, didn't we?" she said, "We did it for our children, for our community."

In 1992 many residents were beginning to question how much longer the festival would continue. Paul Westpheling remarked that the festival had "just about petered out now." He noted that "there have been too many revolutions since that time. Not many people know much about bananas in Fulton today." Citizens of Fulton associated Central America with drugs rather than communism. One citizen remarked that "they are selling more dope than bananas now in Central America." Another saw the heyday of the festival as "before the days of marihuana" when "bananas were the big industry down there." Another resident remembered that "back then, there was more interest in those things. Diplomatic things were different. The Marimba Band was really popular and the music was good. The State Department used to handle international relations. There used to be more of everything, more people involved. Things have changed. Some of those countries may not even be friendly any more."

Fulton's ties with the banana industry in 1992 had atrophied and energy and enthusiasm for the annual festival had run out. It was no longer possible to attract corporate sponsorship from banana companies and the thirtieth annual festival was the last. The banana business ended in Fulton in 1970 when electrically refrigerated railroad cars no longer needed ice. Much of the banana transport had been taken up by tractor-trailer trucks. The railroad no longer employed many people because diesel engines do not need as much attention as steam engines once did. At one time twenty-five passenger trains passed through Fulton a day on the five railroad lines but there is no passenger service to Fulton now. Fulton and South Fulton remain small rural agricultural towns, struggling with empty shops on Main Street and with few employment or cultural opportunities for young people. The banana festival was replaced in the mid-1990s with "Weekend at Pontotoc," a Friday and Saturday event the third weekend in September in the new downtown park named Pontotoc. The features include music, children's games, a barbeque cook-off, and a parade. There is no banana pudding.

8

MEANING OF

Bananas

I T'S CLEAR HOW AND WHY BANANAS became the cheapest fruit in the supermarket and the most widely consumed fruit per capita in the United States. How have bananas become deeply rooted in our culture, in our language, in our songs, jokes, and folklore as well as in our diet? Meanings vary depending on the group using the fruit. Bananas have been a food for slaves, an exotic luxury for the North American wealthy and traveled class, a middle-class luxury, and the poor man's food, traveling a complete circle.

Meaning in culture comes from activity, the cultural applications to which bananas have lent themselves and the uses to which they have been put.[1] The more a part of the culture an item is, the more meanings it will have in different contexts and for different people. Bananas have acquired a number of meanings in the United States; they have been perceived as funny, psychedelic, medicinal, sanitary, decorative, sexual, and the peels as dangers to life and limb. They are also symbols of danger—spiders, snakes, and illegal immigrants—and of romance, of tropical adventure in the Caribbean.

To many people, bananas are inexorably linked with breakfast. Dr. Kellogg's efforts to promote his cereal health foods coincided with a flood of bananas on the American market. Bananas and other fruit make the stuff taste better and easier to swallow, and fruit-company marketing promoted this combination with various forms of advertising. On the packaging of most adult cereals, bowls of cereal with fruit garnishes are displayed, a daily reminder that cereal and fruit "go together." Early advertisements pictured Puffed Wheat or Puffed Rice with bananas as a "morning treat." In 1910 the cereal was shown spooned over a bowl of sliced bananas but soon this scenario was reversed, and bananas were sliced into bowls of cereal instead.[2] In the 1990s new banana-flavored cereals such as Banana Nut Crunch and banana-flavored instant oatmeal appeared on supermarket shelves, obviating the need to slice a fresh banana.[3]

For most of the nineteenth century, bananas were a luxury for the wealthy who could afford to buy the few that made their way to the ports of East Coast cities. Considering where bananas come from and what it takes to get them to the consumer, the fruit is still a luxury. However, Americans eat so much imported food that it no longer makes a difference where an item is from nor how far it has traveled. We expect to find the same selection of fresh fruit and vegetables on the grocery shelves year round. Food is considered a luxury when it is expensive, seasonal, or rare, with raspberries, blueberries, lobster, fancy chocolate, wild game, asparagus, oysters, and wild rice still among the luxurious items that appear seasonally in our supermarkets.

When bananas became the poor man's fruit, they disappeared from the dinner tables of the wealthy. Bananas have never been a selection of the Fruit of the Month Club despite there being over a hundred delicious varieties.[4] Almost everyone likes bananas but no one takes them seriously. They are now considered as plebeian as the hot dog or hamburger, until the 1990s seldom appearing in fancy pastries or elaborate creations unless the gathering was self-consciously "camp." Occasional society parties and fund-raising events—such as the Carmen Miranda Party benefitting the Brooklyn Academy of Music in October 1991 to which several guests wore turbans decorated with plastic fruit—have bananas turned out as a fun theme. At another gala dinner, guests were instructed to pluck the bananas tied to the palm trees around the room and take them to the waiting chefs to be turned into Bananas Foster, a dessert of bananas flamed with rum and brown sugar.

The link between bananas and health was made early and remains strong. The jogging craze in the 1980s brought many people to focus on nutrition in a new way. The consumption of bananas has been promoted for their potassium, fiber, and carbohydrate content. Ironman triathletes, who swim two miles, bicycle a hundred and twelve, and then run a marathon, eat almost nothing but bananas the whole way.[5] In addition to athletes, many older people attribute the daily consumption of bananas to their longevity. When in 1993 the W. B. Doner & Company advertising agency looked for pitch-people for a new campaign for Chiquita Tropical Products, they scouted health clubs and office lobbies. They recruited eighty-year-old Bert Morrow who works out and eats a banana every day as well as Julie Fernando who said that her daily routine included eating a banana and climbing sixteen flights of stairs to her office.[6] One man who celebrated his 105th birthday in 1992 attributed his longevity to eating a banana every day at 11 A.M. His birthday party was "bananas unlimited."[7]

Bananas have a place as comfort food for many people, adults as well as children. Their texture is undemanding and little or no preparation is needed. Many children are fed bananas as their first solid food, and mashed or squished bananas feel good as well as taste good. Despite the ease of preparation and availability of the fruit, baby-food companies produce a wide variety of banana mixtures in little jars to provide even greater convenience to harried parents. Peanut butter and banana sandwiches are popular with older children. Homey desserts such as banana cream pie and banana pudding with vanilla wafers are scoffed at by sophisticated diners, but are welcome friends in small restaurants across the country serving home cooking as well as in supermarket salad bars.

Banana bread has become a symbolic offering. Easy to prepare, homemade banana bread is a hostess gift that is always welcome and is perceived as more personal than a purchased present. Home-made bread also resonates culturally at a time when the majority of women are working outside the household. It is symbolic of a simpler, happier time when mother stayed home. For those who do not bake, the in-store bakeries of major supermarkets also provide loaves of "homemade" banana bread.

Bananas have achieved symbolic importance in other ways. In the nineteenth century, they were associated with missionaries and the people living in the tropics although bananas never gained the importance of the pineapple, the symbol of hospitality. At the turn of the century, banana peels became associated with the "garbage nuisance" in urban areas. As the price of bananas decreased and they became a popular street snack or quick lunch, the peels were tossed into the street or on the sidewalk as was most other garbage and trash. Litter was generally blamed on the people in working-class ethnic neighborhoods but littering was acceptable public behavior by all classes. In most communities, only the main streets and those in fashionable neighborhoods received regular, often private, street cleaning and trash removal service.[8]

The danger of slipping on fruit peels was in fact a notion that predated the proliferation of banana peels in the city. In 1861 a writer for the *Sunday School Advocate,* a weekly newspaper for children, warned his young readers about the dangers of throwing orange or banana peels on the sidewalk:

> Don't do it, boys and girls, unless you want to break somebody's neck. At least a dozen times in my life have I stepped on orange- or banana-peel, slipped up, and wrenched my back in the endeavor to keep on my feet. If I hadn't been quite a spry old gent I should have been thrown flat on my back, perhaps have broken my head, and died of orange-peel thrown on the sidewalk by Master Frank Thoughtless. Haven't I good reason for saying, *Don't throw orange or banana peel on the sidewalk!*

The author went on to relate the story of a man who slipped on an orange peel, broke his leg, was taken to the hospital, had his leg amputated, lost his job, was unable to support his family, and his wife and children ended in the almshouse. "All this sorrow was caused by the bit of orange-peel which Miss Sweet-tooth dropped on the sidewalk. Now do you wonder why I say *don't throw orange or banana peel on the sidewalk?*"[9]

It is likely that most readers of the *Sunday School Advocate* had never seen a banana in 1861. Bananas were extremely rare and oranges were also a luxury at that time. Well-bred children were told that "it is ill-mannered to eat anything in the street. No rubbish, such as paper, nutshells, or orange-peel should be thrown on the sidewalk; there is a proper place for such things; and we ought to have too much regard for the neat appearance of our streets to litter them."[10] Adults were also cautioned in *Harper's Weekly* (1879) that "whosoever throws banana or orange skins on the sidewalk does a great unkindness to the public, and is quite likely to be responsible for a broken limb."[11] A joke published in 1885 went as follows:

> "Sa-ay, Jonnie, wot'll you buy for yer lunch?" said a boot-black to another. "'N orange," was the reply. "High-toned, ain't yer?" said the first. "No," said the other, "but the skins is good to make people fall down with."[12]

Despite sporadic protests against the "garbage nuisance" in the nineteenth century, city streets in the nineteenth century were unspeakably filthy. By the 1890s scavenger pigs had been replaced by men with brooms who were possibly less effectual. City streets were fouled daily by horse manure and urine. Householders and shopkeepers swept their floors into the street and placed their trash, garbage, and the ashes from stoves and fireplaces in uncovered cans and boxes on the curb for pick-up. In addition, dead animals were thrown into the gutter, men spit tobacco juice, and children urinated and defecated on the pavements.[13]

The paving of city streets at the turn of the century created even more of a problem because the refuse could not be absorbed into the road surface. Why people were concerned specifically about fruit peels with all the rest of the mess in the streets is an interesting question. Banana peels appeared in the streets at the same time that a large wave of immigration crowded American cities. As residents became concerned about the growing refuse problem, banana peels may have become a code word for all garbage and litter or even the "immigrant problem" itself.

New York City led the way in civic sanitation efforts. In the nineteenth century, the city police department was responsible for clean streets and was widely accused of appointing men to cleaning jobs who either were unfit to do the work or collected their wages without doing any work at all. In 1878 the New York Municipal Society advocated taking the responsibility away from the police but their efforts were blocked by Tammany Hall.[14] Col. George E. Waring Jr. was appointed Commissioner of Streets on January 15, 1895, and proceeded to clean up the city. Waring was given a free hand to reform the street cleaning service. He did the job along military lines, instilling pride in the men doing the job, requiring them to wear white uniforms, and holding annual parades of uniformed Sanitation Department workers that impressed city residents.

Waring also established Juvenile Street Cleaning Leagues in the schools to enlist children in the campaign to keep the city streets clean. The idea was to instill civic pride in the children and to pass the message to immigrant parents at home, many of whom did not speak English.[15] Children were encouraged to act as the eyes, ears, and noses for the department in discovering unsanitary conditions in their neighborhoods and in identifying the perpetrators. After a slow start, the program became a rousing success. By 1899 there were seventy-five Juvenile Street Cleaning Leagues throughout the city with 5,000 participants. Members held weekly meetings, took a civic pledge to keep from littering the streets, and wore little white caps and official badges.[16]

The children also sang songs such as "And We Will Keep Right On," sung to the tune of the "Battle Hymn of the Republic." The second verse went like this:

No longer will you see a child fall helpless in the street
Because some slippery peeling betrayed his trusting
   feet.
We do what we are able to make our sidewalks neat
And we will keep right on.[17]

The first verse of "Neighbor Mine" specifically mentioned banana peels:

There are barrels in the hallways,
   Neighbor mine;
Pray be mindful of them always,
   Neighbor mine.
If you're not devoid of feeling,
Quickly to those barrels stealing,
Throw in each banana-peeling
   Neighbor mine![18]

Members of the Juvenile League were also expected to make weekly reports on their activities. One child wrote:

Colonel Waring Dear Sir: While walking through Broome
Street, Monday at 2:30 p.m., I saw a man throughing a mattress
on the street. I came over to him and asked him if he had no
other place to put it but there. He told me that he does not no
any other place. So I told him in a barrel, he then picked it up
and thanked me for the inflammation I gave him. I also picked
up 35 banans skins, 43 water mellion shells, 2 bottles and 3
cans and a mattress from Norfolk Street.

Another child reported: "I saw a man eating a banana. He took the skin and threw it on the sidewalk. I said to him please Sir will you be so kind & pick it up and he said all right."[19]

Waring resigned after only three years in office when Tammany came back to power in the city in 1897. The high standards that he set in street cleaning and garbage disposal gradually declined, but the example remained powerful. In 1908 the Juvenile Leagues were revived and a parade and picnic held at Dexter Park, Brooklyn, drew 15,000 children. They marched under a banner inscribed "Clean Streets."[20] Officials from the Department of Street Cleaning once again gave talks on sanitation in public schools and encouraged League activities. In 1912 the department's annual report noted that 1,420 litter cans had been placed "at intervals along the curb for the deposit of litter and fruit skins by pedestrians."[21]

Many other American cities, including Philadelphia, Pittsburgh, Utica, and Denver, followed New York's lead.[22] The Civic Improvement League of Saint Louis issued a set of city ordinances in 1902 "specially applicable to Sidewalks, Streets and Alleys." Section Eleven Hundred and Fifty-Nine entitled "Throwing Fruit on Sidewalks Forbidden" was to be posted in every store, stand, or other place where fruit, vegetables, "or other substance, which, when stepped upon by any person, is liable to cause him or her to slip or fall."[23]

Bananas became symbolic of the new science of city sanitation. Americans were aware of the new yellow fruit peels on city streets in a way that they were oblivious of other, more mundane trash and garbage. Banana peels stood out more than orange peels, and there were probably more of them too. Bananas were easier to eat on the street than oranges or melon—less juicy, easier to peel, and cheap.

Eating bananas in the street was associated with poor people, particularly immigrants, since cultured people were not supposed to eat in public. The lower classes ate the fruit and discarded the peels, endangering their social betters. A two-panel cartoon with the title "Banana-Skin Butcheries" published in *Harper's Weekly* in 1880 showed an Irishman leaning against a wall and dropping a banana peel on the sidewalk in the path of a dignified gentleman wearing a top hat and carrying a cane. The second panel shows the gentleman being carried off on a stretcher, the banana peel still lying on the sidewalk. The two panels are labeled "Cause" and "Effect."[24] The cartoon was published with the joke section but was more a political, anti-immigrant statement than a humorous one.

It is curious that something as homey and insignificant as a discarded fruit peel can cause a complete upset and loss of dignity. The

"Banana-Skin Butcheries" cartoon (*Harper's Weekly*, May 29, 1880), 343.

image of someone slipping on a banana peel is particularly funny when the person is wearing a suit or a uniform—a person in authority. Comedian Phil Silvers felt that slipping on a banana peel was "somehow . . . always funnier than slipping on a cake of soap or a piece of ice. There is something ludicrous about the banana."[25]

Silvers also starred in the film "Top Banana" in which he sang "If you want to be the top banana, you've got to start at the bottom of the bunch." The term "top banana" was introduced into show business jargon by burlesque comedian Harry Steppe in 1927 as a synonym for the top comic on the bill. The term is supposed to have risen from a double-talk routine in which three comics try to share two bananas.[26] Another show business term, "second banana," refers to supporting actresses or actors, or anyone who has a secondary role. When comedian Joey Faye died in 1997, his obituary in *The Economist* hailed him as "among the greatest of second bananas."[27]

Top Banana Game (Waltham, Massachusetts: Thomas P. McCann, 1965).

Jokes, cartoons, poems, and films continue to this day to feature people falling on banana peels, even though banana peels are seldom seen on the sidewalk. The limerick craze that began in the nineteenth century produced several versions of Hannah and the banana. This one, published in 1886, may have been one of the first:

THAT CRUEL BANANA
A certain young woman named Hannah
Slipped down on a piece of banana;
She shrieked, and oh, my'd!
And more stars she spied
Than belong to the star-spangled banner.

A gentleman sprang to assist her,
And picked up her muff and her wrister.
"Did you fall, ma'am?" he cried,
"Do you think," she replied,
"I sat down for the fun of it, Mister?"[28]

Variations of the story of Hannah remained popular and appeared in 1910 and 1926 in published limerick collections.[29]

According to Freud, the jokes of innocence are aimless, based on sound difference or word-play. Jokes of experience express hostility or aggression.[30] Like dreams, they express repressed or unconscious wishes. Another theorist has postulated that at the most primitive level,

> a less flexible, less versatile individual endangers the biolgical integrity of the herd; and so the herd acts to protect itself. We laugh at the man who falls on the banana skin . . . because instead of retaining his versatility, his spontaneity, and his flexibility, the man who tumbles is yielding to the force of gravity and is becoming something like a robot. He is becoming an inflexible object, and at that moment he is being reminded to pull himself together, to restore himself to a state of vigilant flexibility which will then make him into a valuable and productive member of the herd.[31]

Another theory suggests that comedy is a momentary and publicly useful resistance to authority and an escape from its pressures; its mechanism is a free discharge of repressed psychic energy or resentment, through laughter.[32] Pratfalls are usually funny because someone in a position of power or authority, someone in a suit, has taken a fall. We are not laughing from a sense of superiority, but from a subversive, latent aggression. According to Charles Darwin (who wrote a book on the expression of emotion in 1872), "behind the cackle lurks the desire, lurks the intention, to hurt . . . laughter may well be a civilized version of lethal instinct."[33]

Many banana jokes either capitalize on the phallic shape of the fruit or on the notion of slipping on the peel. In 1878 *Harper's Weekly* published one of the first banana jokes: "The older the seeds, the more perfect the lady-slippers will be. And the older the banana peel, the less graceful and the more perfect will be the gentleman slippers."[34] The story of the man with the banana in his ear who apologizes for not being able to hear because of the banana in his ear is an old favorite, popular since the 1940s at least. Raymond Sokolov suggests that "it is the kind of humorous, cryptosexual joke Freud would have said made us laugh because it relieved the tension and fear that sex and sexually symbolic objects induce."[35] In 1966 in response to a revival of Chiquita Banana singing her calypso antirefrigeration song, a seven-year-old submitted the following schoolyard parody to United Fruit: "I'm Chiquita Banana and I'm here to say if you want to get rid of your teacher the easy way, just peel a banana, put the peel on the floor, and watch your teacher slide out the door."[36]

Not all banana peel jokes are hostile. Charles Lamb, early in the nineteenth century, suggested that "laughter is an overflow of sympathy, an amiable feeling of identity with what is disreputably human, a relish for the whimsical, the odd, the private blunder."[37] The humor theory of sympathy/empathy contradicts the theories of derision/superiority and disappointment/frustrated expectation.[38] There is a distinction between humor and mockery; humor is found in a contrast between the thing as it is or ought to be, and the thing smashed out of shape and as it ought not to be, like a broken umbrella that looks "funny."[39] Banana peel jokes continue to circulate. "You may be a fine, upstanding citizen, but that makes no difference to a banana peel" was cited in the *New Yorker* in 1973.[40] Recently a child asked her piano teacher, "Why is a banana peel like music? If you don't C sharp you'll B flat."

Bananas can be fun to talk with. The word itself is reiterative and fun to say—like the joke "I can spell banana, I just don't know when to stop." Another example is Shirley Ellis's song "The Name Game," a popular hit in the 1960s, much to the dismay of many hearing it for the twentieth or thirtieth time. Another example of current children's humor is the knock-knock joke:

> Knock knock . . . Who's there?
> Banana . . . Banana who? . . . [repeat]
> Knock knock . . . Who's there?

Orange . . . Orange who?
Orange you glad I didn't say banana?

Bananas can lend themselves to wonderful puns such as that great
swing band of the 1930s, Willie Bananas and His Bunch—The Band
with A-Peel.[41] A 1993 advertisement for the International Ladies
Garment Worker's Union featured a 1940s' poster that proclaimed
"Stick to your union bunch or you'll get skinned!" The poster also
showed an enormous hand of fifteen bananas. The modern caption
reads "Going Bananas about Education."[42]

Stephen Leacock claims that the language of humor defies trans-
lation, putting a barrier between cultures, particularly as most humor deals with fragmentary, topical allusions to current events.[43]
Former banana republics now caught up with fighting drug traffic
are perceived as threatening rather than funny, which may explain
why there are few banana jokes in circulation. Garrison Keeler's
joke show that aired on the radio program "Prairie Home Companion" in the spring of 1996 had no banana jokes in the entire
two-hour segment.

In countries where bananas are grown, they are taken much more
seriously. Bananas represent hard work and the basis of the family
income, and the people do not tell banana jokes or slip up on banana peels.[44] In the United States, the connection between banana
peels and pratfalls has become a standard theme for cartoonists.
The banana peel is comic when it is ubiquitous and cheap, and
there is no intrinsic value attached to it. A comic postcard post-
marked Chicago 1909 pictures a man with a top hat slipping on a
banana peel with a woman laughing at him in the background. The
caption reads: "I will write when I get on my feet." A Mutt and Jeff
cartoon from 1914 featured Jeff slipping on a banana peel.[45]
Banana-peel pratfalls continue to be a cartoonist's stock-in-trade,
appearing in the 1990s in Garfield, B.C., Hagar the Horrible,
Broom Hilda, Beetle Bailey, Ralph, Ziggy, the Fusco Brothers,
Mother Goose and Grimm, Speed Bump, and Gary Larson's work,
among others.[46] No matter how often they are used, the banana

"I will write when I get on my feet," postcard (1906).

peel is still funny. Even modern children's books use the pratfall.
One of the illustrations in *Maxi, The Hero* shows a purse-snatcher
who slipped on a banana peel on the steps of the entrance to a sub-
way station.[47]

The *Reader's Digest* and other compendiums of gravestone humor have published an epitaph attributed to Enosburg, Vermont, that reads:

> Here lies the body of our Anna
> Done to death by a banana.
> It wasn't the fruit that laid her low
> But the skin of the thing that made her go.[48]

Unfortunately a search of seven graveyards in Enosburg County failed to find the stone. The local historical society has also been unable to locate it so the epitaph is probably apocryphal. The notion of the danger of banana peels is so much a part of our culture that the idea of dying from a fall is humorous but also easily acceptable. There are also reports of passengers bringing successful lawsuits against railroad companies for bodily injuries sustained by slipping and falling on banana skins.[49] The author of *Accidentally, On Purpose: The Making of a Personal Injury Underworld in America* claims that F. E. Caldwell made his living in the 1920s by riding in railcars and slipping on banana peels that he had carefully tossed at his own feet. "Though he was never prosecuted, some of the many 'banana-peelers' he inspired did hard time."[50] The idea of slipping on a banana peel is also expressed in the wry expression used when life seems to be falling apart: to have one foot in the grave and the other on a banana peel.

Records of banana peel pratfalls in vaudeville routines are hard to find, although a few did include bananas. Annette Kellermann, famous for swimming the English channel and known as the Million Dollar Mermaid, ate a banana underwater in a tank on stage as part of her act. In the 1950s Florida's Weeki Wachee Spring of the Mermaids near Brooksville offered tourists an underwater show where "two of the lovely talented Mermaids will thrill you with their awe-inspiring performance" including eating bananas underwater.[51] This was an impressive physical feat with strong phallic overtones.

A. Robbins was a clown with a novelty act in which he would take a seemingly endless number of bananas out of his pockets. *The Bill-board* noted in 1930 that it was "a sure-fire act."[52] Robbins took his act to television in the 1950s, appearing as the banana man on the Ed Sullivan show and later the children's show "Captain Kangaroo." Robbins wore a baggy suit and a clown wig of straight hair. He never spoke but uttered a high-pitched wail while pulling bananas from every pocket in his suit, and squares of cardboard that he opened to make boxes. When he finished, there would be three boxes resembling freight train cars which would be full of bananas. Then the suit was turned into a train engineer's outfit and he would chug off stage.[53] Another vaudevillian, George L. Rockwell, known as Dr. Rockwell, Quack, Quack, Quack, gave a lecture on the human anatomy using a banana stalk as a skeleton.

Banana pratfalls appeared in silent films such as *Banana Skins* (1908) and *The Passing of a Grouch* (1910), and talking pictures such as *Sherlock Jr.* (1924) and *The Cameraman* starring Buster Keaton. In *Banana Skins* a street vendor sells a hand of bananas to a mother and child and they are followed by the camera as they discard banana peels along the route for others to slip on. *The Passing of a Grouch* begins with a man slipping on a banana peel on the way to the office. The rest of his day is one long series of mishaps.

Humor also plays with inverted situations: we enjoy the surprise of expecting the same joke and finding it reversed. Clowning is funnier when the tricks seem to fail. Slapstick comedy uses caricature, exaggerated action, and overdramatization as in the *Sherlock Jr.* film where Buster Keaton lays a trap for a rival with a banana peel, and then forgets and slips on it himself. We anticipate the fall of the villain, then laugh when the hero entraps himself. *Hit the Ice* (1943) with Bud Abbott and Lou Costello includes a scene where Costello pulls a banana out of his pocket instead of a gun. We laugh at incongruity, at frustrated expectations. In addition, this was a parody of Mae West's famous line, "Is that a pistol in your pocket or are you glad to see me?" One of the highlights of a more recent film, *It's a Mad, Mad, Mad, Mad World,* featured Ethel Merman slipping on a banana peel.

When the song "Yes, We Have No Bananas" by Frank Silver and Irving Cohn achieved enormous popularity in 1923, selling at a rate of 25,000 copies a day, some flappers and their beaus carefully danced the Charleston on banana-peel strewn dance floors.[54] Banana peels were used as a symbol of defiance against the establishment concerns for safety and order. The song's popularity enabled Frank Silver to tour the country with a "Banana Band" for several years. The musicians wore gold costumes and performed on daises decorated with glittery banana cutouts.[55] "Yes! We Have No Bananas" was featured in the 1930 movie *Mammy*, starring Al Jolson with music and lyrics by Irving Berlin.

Current banana-peel jokes no longer appear to be actuated by feelings of hostility; rather, the humor arises from feelings of empathy. Life is unsure, a pratfall may lie just around the corner, you may be the one to slip up next, and pratfalls are no longer funny if anyone gets hurt. James Thurber suggests that "the things we laugh at are awful while they are going on but funny when we look back. And other people laugh because they've been through it, too."[56]

Are banana skins really a hazard to pedestrians? They decay rapidly and are only potentially slippery when freshly discarded. They are also large and rather obvious when lying on a sidewalk. The banana skin pratfall has become an important comic element in our culture but few people claim to have slipped on one themselves or actually know of someone who has fallen. The idea is funny—because it is so improbable?

Obscene wit is sexual exhibition and the banana serves as a ready symbol because of its phallic associations.[57] Although William Safire suggests that Americans find bananas amusing—"a sunny yellow curved in the shape of a smile, as if to say, 'Have a Nice Day' "— bananas are frankly phallic.[58] The size and shape of the banana may explain its exclusion from polite dining room art in the nineteenth century, although humorous paintings did include bananas. A pair of paintings depicting monkeys destroying a dining room in the process of raiding a bowl of fruit containing bananas was painted by Henry Church of Chagrin Falls, Ohio, between 1895 and 1900. Another of a dog and a monkey in a dining room was painted by Robert Walter Weir who died in 1887. These humorous paintings relied on the contrast between the dining room as it is, or ought to be, and the wreckage caused by an almost human agent. Banana paintings represent suppressed hostility at social control and the conventions of polite society as they are usually played out in the dining room.

Josephine Baker, an American jazz dancer in Paris, took the city by storm in 1924 wearing nothing but a belt of glittering bananas and a pearl necklace during her performance.[59] Another exotic singer and dancer, Carmen Miranda (known as the Brazilian Bombshell), was imported from Rio in 1939 as part of Hollywood's propaganda efforts for Roosevelt's Good Neighbor Policy with Latin America.[60] She became one of the highest-paid performers in Hollywood in the 1940s and was immensely popular in the United States until her career went into a decline in the 1950s. She wore flamboyant costumes with a bare midriff, occasionally sported headdresses or hats with tropical fruit motifs, and recorded the hit song "Bananas Is My Business." In the 1943 Busby Berkeley film *The Gang's All Here,* featuring Miranda, a scene in a Broadway nightclub decorated as a banana grove included barrel organ players, performing monkeys, and a chorus line of beautiful women carrying huge bananas with overtly phallic symbolism. At one point, they sit on the ground waving the giant bananas which they hold between their legs while Miranda sings "The Lady in the Tutti Fruitti Hat." The climax to this scene is an explosion of bananas from Carmen Miranda's head.[61] One of Miranda's hit songs was "I Make My Money with Bananas."

The ubiquitous banana split, a combination of a banana and several scoops of ice cream topped with sauce and whipped cream, can be seen as an erotic creation, traditionally shared by teenaged couples as in Louis Prima's recording of the song "Banana Split for My Baby." Images of women eating bananas are also considered slightly risque or in bad taste. Amy Vanderbilt recommended that, except at picnics, bananas should be peeled and then broken up "as needed into small pieces" and "conveyed to the mouth with the fin-

Unidentified photograph of young women eating bananas, n.d.

gers."[62] Jay Leno, television host of the *Tonight Show,* had fun insisting that a reluctant woman guest peel and eat a banana as he interviewed the curator of the California banana museum in July 1995.
In many high school sex education classes, bananas are used to
demonstrate condom use.

In addition to the dangers of slipping on banana peels and the
erotic connotations of the fruit, many people associate bananas
with spiders and snakes. Tarantulas, small snakes, and other creatures are found in the bunches of bananas cut in the tropics, or at
least were common before the widespread use of pesticides. In 1885
readers of the weekly newspaper *The Cook* were cautioned:

> Mrs. B—, City—. We have published recipes for the cooking of
> bananas. Refer to your file of *The Cook*. It will be most economi-
> cal to buy them by the bunch for so large a family, and if they
> are not "dead ripe" when you get them, they will keep quite
> well as long as necessary. But take care that no tarantulas, scor-

pions or centipedes are hidden in the bunch as they very frequently are.[63]

An article in *Popular Science* in 1894 noted that "we shudder at dreadful stories of venomous tarantulas and scorpions lurking in those compact clusters."[64] Ten years later, an article in *Scientific American* stated that "it is not unusual for snakes, tarantulas, and similar unpleasant customers to find a lodging in a bunch of bananas and when discovered at the loading point, the fact 'snake in this car' is usually chalked on the outside, and the carriers handle the bunches very gingerly at the wharf."[65] Tarantulas were popularly known as banana spiders and a 1946 article in *Nature* magazine identified them as "the poisonous spider often found in bunches of bananas when they are shipped to this country."[66] Refrigeration during shipping simply caused the stowaways to hibernate, waking up when the fruit reached room temperature. In attempts to kill the unwanted creatures, ship holds were made air tight and pumped full of gases.[67] One of the favorite stories of a veterinarian in Connecticut in the 1950s was of receiving a small boa constrictor found in a banana ship in New Haven harbor. The snake escaped and he and his wife turned the house upside down looking for it. Several weeks later, the snake was found curled up in the springs of their bed.

The practice of boxing hands of bananas instead of shipping the fruit on the stalk, as well as dipping the fruit in acid to wash off pesticide residue, pretty well eliminated the possibility of tropical insects and snakes being found by North American consumers. Yet the association still remains strong for many Americans forty years later. The cartoonist Gary Larson has an image of two tarantulas sitting in a living room with the caption "It's a letter from Julio in America. . . . His banana bunch arrived safely and he's living in the back room of some grocery store."[68] Larson turned the concept upside down with a cartoon of poodles sticking out of bunches of bananas being unloaded from a ship with the caption "How poodles first came to North America."[69] The association remains strong in our folklore despite the fact that there probably hasn't been a stowaway since the 1960s. This brainteaser was published in *Parade Magazine* in 1993:

> There are three boxes in a South American warehouse—one marked "Tarantulas," one marked "Bananas," and the third marked "Tarantulas and Bananas." You are told that all three boxes are marked wrong, and you must rearrange the labels correctly. Without peeking, you may withdraw only one item from each box. What is the minimum number of boxes from which you would have to remove an item in order to be able to correctly label all three?[70]

The other creature associated with bananas is the monkey. Despite the fact that many monkeys do not have bananas available to them in the wild, bananas are widely believed to be the basis of their diet. The association may have begun with Italian organ grinders who provided street entertainment that often included a monkey to attract children. Popular imagination may have conflated them with the Italian fruit vendors who also had pushcarts and were frequently seen in the city streets. Chimpanzees and apes are often portrayed with bananas. In the 1964 Ray Drusky hit song "Peel Me a Nanner," the lyrics included

> Peel me a nanner, toss me a peanut
> I'll come a-swingin' from a coconut tree
> Peel me a nanner, toss me a peanut
> You sure made a monkey out of me.[71]

The *New Dictionary of American Slang* states that "to go bananas" comes from the spectacle of monkeys or apes greedily gobbling bananas.[72] When someone "goes bananas," they are said to be acting as crazy as a monkey. In a "B.C." cartoon, "go bananas" is defined as "the rallying cheer at chimpanzee tech."[73] Bananas and monkeys are another favorite topic for cartoonists. Mike Twohy shows two gorillas looking at a discarded banana peel with the caption "Thank God no one was hurt!"[74] Bud Grace drew a visit to the doctor by a man with a bad back. He can't straighten up so the doctor recommends eating a bunch of bananas so that he will be able to pass for a gorilla.[75] After Dennis the Menace asks Mr. Wilson why he isn't growing bananas in his garden, Mr. Wilson calls Dennis a little monkey.[76] Gary Larson used animal characters in his cartoons to expose human foibles. In one an ape says, "You know, Sid, I really like bananas . . . I mean, I know that's not profound or nothin' . . . Heck! We all do. But for me, I thinks it goes much more beyond that." Monkeys are seen as sharing basic human instincts without the constraints of civilization.

Ben and Jerry's banana-flavored Chunky Monkey ice cream perpetuates the association between bananas and monkeys, as does the packaging for Safeway-brand Frosted Flakes breakfast cereal that features a monkey as well as a bowl of cereal with slices of banana. Newspaper advertisements for Disney's 1997 film *George of the Jungle* featured a man and an ape each holding a giant banana.[77] Richard Scarry's *Floating Bananas,* a Little Golden Book published in 1993, features Bananas Gorilla driving his bananamobile to the harbor where he finds a banana ship unloading bunches of bananas. He is suspected of being a banana thief but turns out to be a cook who produces banana soup for the whole crew of gorillas. This book contains all the banana cliches except slipping on a peel. Monkeys and bananas are associated in the American mind with tropical climates. But somehow monkeys and mangoes or monkeys and papayas do not seem as funny. Perhaps it is the phallic associations of the banana that make this pairing humorous.

Phallic associations are spelled out in songs such as "I Wanna Put My Banana in Your Fruit Basket" recorded by Bo Carter in 1931, "Please Don't Squeeza da Banana" by Louis Prima, "Banana Man Blues" sung by Memphis Minnie in 1934, and "My Wife Left Town with a Banana" by Carlos Borzini, Senior. Other banana songs that have been enjoyed by twentieth-century Americans include "I Like Bananas Because They Have No Bones" recorded by Perry Weeks

"I Like Bananas Because They Have No Bones"
sheet music (New York: Crawford Music Corporation, 1936).

and his orchestra in 1936, "30,000 Pounds of Bananas" by Harry
Chapin, "The Name Game" by Shirley Ellis, and "Chiquita Banana"
by the King Sisters (1946), among others. In 1959 Harry Belafonte
popularized "The Banana Boat Song" or "Day-O" as it is sometimes
called. This was a calypso song about loading bananas onto ships at
night. This song may have marked the peak of the popularity of
United Fruit. It was widely sung by folksingers and parodied on a
recording by Stan Freberg. The song also was featured on the *Mup-
pet Show* on television in the early 1980s. [See Appendix for a list of
banana songs.]

Children's singers have found bananas to be a reliable motif.

Raffi recorded "Apples and Bananas" and "Bananaphone" (1994), and Barry Louis Polisar sang "My Brother Thinks He's a Banana" in 1977. "Bananas in Pajamas" was recorded by B1 and B2. Some more recent banana songs include "I'm Going Bananas" by Madonna (1990), "Banana Love" by the Bobs (1987), "God's Great Banana Skin" by Chris Rea (1993), and "Banana Bobine" by The Rebels (1989). One of the oddest in this group of strange songs was "Japanese Banana" recorded by the Chipmunks about the unavailability of bananas in Japan.[78]

In the late 1960s, the banana became a counterculture symbol. According to Freud, humor, like dreams, expresses repressed or unconscious wishes.[79] In April 1967 *Newsweek* reported that banana-peel smoking for a psychedelic high had "touched off a banana-buying boom from the Haight-Asbury district to Harvard Square."[80] It was alleged to produce hallucinogenic states similar to LSD.[81] The recipe for preparing banana peels for smoking, which began as a satire in the *Berkeley Barb* in March, was picked up and reprinted by New York City's *East Village Other*, the *Village Voice*, as well as the *Los Angeles Free Press*. According to *Time* magazine, "Banana-heads scrape the white fibers from the inside of the peel, boil the scrapings into a paste, which is then baked. The dark brown ash that results is smoked in hand-rolled cigarette 'joints' or in pipes, tastes vaguely like a burning compost heap."[82]

The wonderful thing about bananas was that they were legal. Large banana symbols were carried to the Easter Sunday 1967 Be-in in New York's Central Park where the crowd chanted "Ba-nan-a! Ba-nan-a! Ba-nan-a!"[83] United Fruit stickers from supermarket bananas became cool additions to school notebooks. T-shirts appeared with the blue United Fruit Company seal. The British pop singer Donovan's song "Mellow Yellow" was a popular hit, and the record album cover of The Velvet Underground & Nico produced by Andy Warhol featured a green banana cut-out that peeled off to reveal a pink/orange fruit.

United Fruit took fright at this new image for its bananas and countered the psychedelic claims with an extensive testing program by the Federal Drug Administration and scientists at the University of California at Los Angeles and at New York University.[84] Some chemists suggested that bananas contained serotonin, a neurochemical closely related to hallucinogenic chemicals, such as psilocybin and dimethyltryptamine, that might possibly trigger genuine physiological effects under combustion.[85]

It turned out that banana peel smoking was a joke, although many teenagers tried it. It got a wonderful reaction from the establishment who were hard put to try to regulate the possession of banana peels in the same way as marihuana and LSD. As the *Village Voice* pointed out, "What legislator would dare affix his name to the Banana Control Act of 1968?"[86] The issue even found its way to Congress when Frank Thompson, a Democrat from New Jersey, humorously (?) proposed a banana-labeling act to halt what he termed an invasion of the fruit stand by a generation of thrill seekers. "From Bananas," intoned Thompson, "it is a short but shocking step to other fruits. Today, the cry is 'burn, banana, burn.' Tomorrow we may face strawberry smoking, dried apricot inhaling, or prune puffing."[87]

The banana as psychedelic symbol faded from the national scene with the decline of the hippie movement and the drug culture in the 1970s although it resurfaced in 1988 in "Smokin' Banana Peels," recorded by the Dead Milkmen. It was significant because it mocked the establishment so well in terms of international companies and charges of colonialism in Central America at the time of a colonial-style war in Vietnam.

The notion of a banana republic included images of warm, sunny, tropical islands, deserted beaches, bikini bathing suits, palm trees, and a slow-paced exotic way of life. Americans who went to work for the international banana companies lived better than they could have at home with the benefit of inexpensive servants, country clubs, and other company privileges. Expanding banana plantations into the jungle was an exciting idea to those who had never visited the tropics. Special clothes were necessary, different from those worn to work in most areas of the United States.

The cruises offered by United Fruit and the Standard Fruit and Steamship Company took American tourists to resort areas developed by the companies themselves. In the era before World War II when most Americans did not have paid vacations, the idea of taking a month off for a cruise was only a dream. Banana company plantations were the setting for many short stories in popular magazines, such as the *Saturday Evening Post,* that fueled these dreams with descriptions of jungles and beaches, desperate outlaws, and dangerous working conditions, coupled with beautiful, scantily clad women, romantic encounters, and easy living.

Carmen Miranda personified the exotic, romantic aspects of the tropics. She frequently wore outrageous headdresses complete with tropical fruit and flowers and danced sensuously in exotic costumes that bared her midriff. In 1995 a documentary of the life of Carmen Miranda, with the title "Bananas Is My Business," was released in the United States. Although she had no connection with United Fruit or other companies, in the minds of most Americans she was closely connected with bananas through the image of Chiquita Banana.

In 1952 Butterick published a pattern for a Chiquita Banana costume in children's and misses' sizes: "Just follow the simplified pattern for the dress and hat, and you'll have a costume that will set you dancing the mambo."[88] The advertisement included a United Fruit Company seal depicting Chiquita Banana copyright 1947. There was no bare midriff shown in the picture. The costume consisted of a long full skirt with a long sash, a scooped neck blouse with puffed short sleeves, and a broad brimmed hat that tilted up to hold imitation fruit or flowers. It bore little resemblance to Carmen Miranda's costumes but it did look a bit like the Chiquita Banana advertising character. McCall's published a Chiquita Banana dress and hat pattern in 1966 that was very popular for Halloween that year.[89]

Another iteration of the notion of romantic adventure in the tropics is the chain of stores in the United States named "Banana Republic" that sells cruise and vacation clothing. The stores are often decorated with a safari or jungle theme and have been highly

Chiquita Banana Costume Pattern
(McCall's Pattern 101, n.d.).

successful. Most customers probably will not travel to a jungle for vacation but the clothes are popular for weekends in the wilds of Connecticut or Virginia. Other banana products that hold out a promise of romantic tropical adventure include inflatable bananas for the home swimming pool. A "tropical banana pool lounge" consisting of three five-foot-long banana fingers offered two extra-large drink holders.[90] Many mail-order companies provide one-person banana boats, and floating, inflatable tropical islands complete with palm tree and giant banana to recline against.

Two people have become so interested in bananas in American

Banana Hat and Frill Bag pattern (New York: Jensen
Creation 3, Heirloom Needlework Guild, 1944).

culture that they have created banana museums, one in California, the other in Washington State. Ann Lovell of Auburn, Washington, has amassed nearly 3,000 items, including a banana-shaped, four-foot high, bass stringed instrument, banana cookbooks, movies, songs, salt and pepper shakers, clothing, jewelry, stuffed animals and dolls, and other banana-shaped objects.[91] Her collection was featured on *The Collectibles Show* on the FX channel, July 11, 1995, and in the Fall 1996 issue of *Collectibles*.

The second museum is located in Altadena, California, and is curated by Ken Bannister. His collection is said to include 15,000 items categorized in five sections: hard, featuring such items as a glass banana; soft, including stuffed bananas, oven mitts, and leather banana coats to keep bananas warm in winter; food, including banana-flavored popcorn; clothing, including banana-shaped slippers and banana-print boxer shorts; and a library of banana books.[92] In 1972 Bannister organized an international banana club with 8,000 members from 45 states and 13 countries. Members received a banana pin, bumper sticker, banana patch, membership card, and an invitation to an annual picnic in Arcadia, California. "Bananas keep people smiling," says Bannister, 45. "Would you join a raisin club?"[93]

Banana-eating was not a habit acquired from the people of Central America or Africa. Banana consumption in the United States was a marketing success largely attributable to United Fruit Company. Americans have long been a fruit-loving people, and bananas have been incorporated into the national diet in combination with and in place of other seasonal fruit. Bananas are interchangeable with many other fruits on cereal and in desserts; they are simply cheaper and available all the time.

Other imported fruit such as the kiwi, star fruit, and mango remain expensive, seasonal, and generally available in limited quantities. They are also harder to eat. Bananas are easy to peel, sanitary, bland, and have no treacherous seeds or pits. The only drawback to bananas is that the fruit discolors quickly when exposed to the air.

At the turn of the century, bananas were incorporated into the daily lives of many Americans with unusual rapidity. Sidney Mintz suggests that "in any culture, these processes of assimilation are also ones of appropriation: the culture's way of making new and unusual things part of itself."[94] As bananas were assimilated into the diet in the United States, they were also being appropriated as American. Banana drinks such as Melzo and recipes for cooked bananas with meatloaf were unsuccessful but banana splits, banana bread, and bananas in combination with other fruit or in more traditional fruit desserts continue to expand the market. Fulton, Kentucky, was able to claim to be the Banana Capital of the World and bananas have taken an undisputed place in the songs, jokes, and folklore of the United States.

It remains to be seen whether Americans will continue to incorporate bananas into their daily diet in additional ways. Plantains and other varieties of bananas are more common in urban supermarkets with the recent influx of Central American and African immigrants, and they appear on the menus of ethnic restaurants. Some Americans are beginning to examine the impact of their food choices on the people who grow the bananas, and the worldwide food network that is dominated by political and commercial interests. Banana-growing changed the landscape of Central America and the Caribbean, both in terms of ecological change from rain forest to plantation, and in terms of population shifts as thousands of workers recruited by the banana companies migrated from the islands in the Caribbean to the Central American mainland with and without their families. Today there is growing concern that the herbicides and pesticides used on the banana plantations are having an adverse affect on the people who work and live there, and may even be carried to the consumer. Organic bananas are now available in health food stores and banana imports are more carefully scrutinized for chemical residues. But most people in the United States do not think about or care where their food comes from as long as it is inexpensive and readily available. Bananas are funny, sexy, nutritious, and healthy, as "American" as apple pie and strawberry shortcake.

SONGS OF

Bananas

"A Bunch of Bananas"
Performed by Rosemary Clooney

"A Shoe with No Lace, Banana
without a Skin"
Performed live by The Kinks;
never recorded

"All the Nations Like Bananas"
Performed by Charlotte Diamond
(1992)

"Ape Man"
Performed by The Kinks (1970)

"Apples and Bananas"
Performed by Connie Regan and
Barbara Freeman

"Banana"
Performed by Joe King Carrasco
(1987), Banda Bianco, Hot Pink
Turtles, Grupo Mancotal, The
Nelories

"Banana Banana"
Performed by King Kurt (1984)

"Banana Bobine"
Performed by The Rebels (1989)

"Banana Boat"
Performed by Harry Belafonte
(1959), Joe Higgs (1960s), Stan
Freberg (1960s), The Kinks

"Bananafishbone"
Performed by The Cure

"Banana in Your Fruit Basket"
Performed by Bo Carter (1931)

"Banana Jam"
Performed by Cabo Frio (1987)

"Banana Leaf"
Performed by Shonen Knife

"Banana Love"
Performed by The Bobs (1987)

"Banana Man"
Performed by Clifton Chenier

"Banana Man Blues"
Performed by Memphis Minnie
(1934)

"Bananaphone"
Performed by Raffi (1994)

"Banana Republics" by Steve
Goodman
Performed by Steve Goodman,
The Boomtown Rats, Jimmy
Buffett

"Banana Slug"
Performed by The Banana Slug
Band

"Banana Split for My Baby"
Performed by Louis Prima

"Banana Split Republic"
Performed by The False Prophets

"Bananas"
Performed by Louis Jordan (1955)

"Bananas in Pajamas"
Performed by B1 and B2

"Boiled Bananas and Carrots"
Performed by Peter Sellers

"Broadway Banana"
Performed by Linda Arnold
(1991)

"Chiquita Banana"
Performed by the King Sisters
(1946), Buddy Clark, Xavier
Cugat (1950s), Mitch Miller
(1950s)

"God's Great Banana Skin"
Performed by Chris Rea (1993)

"Guabi Guabi"
Performed by George Sibandi

"Have a Banana"
Performed by Plum Tree (c. 1994)

"I Like Bananas Because They
Have No Bones" by Chris
Yacich
Performed by The Hoosier Hot
Shots (1940s), Parry Weeks and
His Orchestra (1936)

"I Make My Money with Bananas"
Performed by Carmen Miranda

"I'm Chiquita Banana"
Radio advertisement (1950s)

"I'm Going Bananas"
Performed by Madonna (1990)

"I've Got Those Yes We Have No
Bananas Blues," words by Lew
Brown, music by James F.
Hanley and Robert King (1937)
Performed by Bailey's Lucky Seven

"I've Never Seen a Straight
Banana"
Performed by The Happiness
Boys; Ted Waite (1926)

"Japanese Banana"
Performed by The Chipmunks

"Loving You Has Made Me
Bananas"
Performed by Gary (or Guy)
Marks (1970s)

"Mellow Yellow"
Performed by Donovan
 (1960s)

"Montana Banana"
Performed by David Newman
 (1991)

"My Brother Thinks He's a
 Banana"
Performed by Barry Louis Polisar
 (1977)

"My Wife Left Town with a
 Banana"
Performed by Carlos Borzini
 Senior

"912 Greens"
Performed by Ramblin' Jack Elliott
 (c. 1967)

"Ode to the Banana King (Part I)"
Performed by Tori Amos

"One Banana, Two Banana"
Performed by The Banana Splits;
 The Dickies

"Phillips Goes Bananas"
Performed by Hound Dog Taylor
 (1982)

"Please Don't Squeeza Da Banana"
Performed by Louis Prima

"Smoking Banana Peels"
Performed by The Dead Milkmen
 (1988)

"Sookie Sookie"
Performed by Don Covay;
 Steppenwolf

"Sweet Talking Man"
Performed by Ruth Wallis

"Talking Green Beret, New Super
 Yellow Hydraulic Banana Blues"
Performed by Jamie Brockett

"The Banana Song"
Performed by The Circle with a
 Smile (1993)

"The Name Game"
Performed by Shirley Ellis (1960s)

"There's a Banana in the Woods
 over There"
Performed by The Love Children

"30,000 Lbs. of Bananas"
Performed by Harry Chapin
 (1970s)

"Two Ladies in the Shade of the
 Banana Tree"
Performed by Pearl Bailey

"Vendedor de Bananas"
Performed by Jorge Ben (1976)

"When Banana Skins Are Falling"
Performed by Slim Gaillard

"When Can I Have a Banana
 Again?"
Performed by Harry Roy and His
 Orchestra

"Why Are Bananas Picked Green?"
Performed by Tom Glazer and
 Paul (Mr. Imagination) Tripp

"Wurds"
Performed by George Carlin
 (1975)

"Yes! We Have No Bananas" by
   Frank Silver and Irving Cohen
Performed by Billy Jones (1923),
   Enoch Light and His Charleston
   City All Stars, Spike Jones and
   His City Slickers, Mitch Miller
   (1950s)

NOTES

INTRODUCTION

1. Jennifer K. Ruark, "A Place at the Table," *Chronicle of Higher Education* 45:44 (July 9, 1999), A17.
2. Sidney W. Mintz, *Sweetness and Power: The Place of Sugar in Modern History* (New York: Elizabeth Seaton Books/Viking, 1985), 6.
3. Lucy Fitch Perkins, *The Filipino Twins* (Cambridge: Riverside Press, 1923).
4. Jane Nickerson, "Bananas—Cooked," *New York Times Magazine* (September 14, 1947), 42.
5. "Three Thousand Million Bananas a Year," *Review of Reviews, American* 44 (July 1911), 99.
6. "The Banana You Know and Love May Be in Considerable Danger," *Wall Street Journal* (April 10, 1995), A13.
7. Stephanie Witt Sedgwick, "Yes! We Have Nice Bananas," *Washington Post* (February 3, 1999), F2.
8. Lance Jungmeyer, "Eating Trends," *The Packer* (December 2, 1996), 6A.
9. *Bananas* (Washington, D.C.: Pan American Union, 1956), 5.
10. B. Roueche, "The Humblest Fruit," *New Yorker* 49 (October 1, 1973), 48.

1. INTRODUCING BANANAS

1. Norman C. Bezona, "Bananas for Southern Gardens," *Horticulture* 41 (July 1963), 374.
2. John F. Mariani, *The Dictionary of American Food and Drink* (New Haven and New York: Ticknor & Fields, 1983), 24; Roueche, "The Humblest Fruit," 44.
3. J. R. Magness, "Fruit of the Wise Men," *National Geographic Magazine* 100 (September 1951), 358; *Bananas* (Washington, D.C.: Pan American Union, 1956), 3.
4. Roueche, "The Humblest Fruit," 44; Mariani, *The Dictionary of American Food and Drink*, 24.
5. *Bananas*, 3; Magness, "Fruit of the Wise Men," 358.
6. Angela M. Fraser, Ph.D., "Plantain," in the National Food Safety Database, http://www.foodsafety.org/nc/nc1057.htm. This is part of "The Notebook of Food and Food Safety Information," produced by the North Carolina Cooperative Extension Service, revised in 1997.
7. "Bananas: Production in Latin America," *Americas* 24 (May 1972 supplement), 21; Claire Shaver Haughton, *Green Immigrants: The Plants That Transformed America* (New York: Harcourt Brace Jovanovich, 1978), 31; Roueche, "The Humblest Fruit," 4.
8. Exhibition label, Museo Nacional de Antropología, Mexico City.
9. Magness, "Fruit of the Wise Men," 358.
10. Marina Warner, *No Go the Bogeyman: Scaring, Lulling, and Making Mock* (New York: Farrar, Straus and Giroux, 1998), 360.
11. "Cover This Month," *Natural History* 55 (September 1946), 299.
12. Magness, "Fruit of the Wise Men," 358; Shannon Brownlea, "The Best Banana Bred," *Atlantic* 264 (September 1989), 28.
13. Brownlea, "The Best Banana Bred," 28.
14. Janet McKenzie Hill, ed., *A Short History of the Banana and a Few Recipes for Its Use* (Boston: United Fruit, 1904), 4.
15. Mabel E. Shepherd, "All about Bananas," *Horticulture* 42 (February 1964), 36; Alexander F. Skutch, "Plant of Paradoxes," *Nature Magazine* 12 (November 1928), 314; Charles Morrow Wilson, "Green Dragon of the Tropics," *Scientific American* 162 (April 1940), 199; "Cover This Month," 299; Middle America Information Bureau, *Middle America and Bananas* (New York: United Fruit, 1946/47), 1.
16. John Wilcock, "About: Bananas," *New York Times Magazine* (March 30, 1958), 53.

17. Bezona, "Bananas for Southern Gardens," 374; "Nothing Says Jungle Quite Like Banana," *Sunset* 156 (June 1976), 78; Richard Langer, "Going Bananas" *House & Garden* 154 (April 1982), 68.

18. Hill, ed., *A Short History of the Banana and a Few Recipes for Its Use*, 3.

19. George L. Austin, *Dr. Austin's Indispensable Hand-Book and General Educator* (Portland, Maine: George Stinson, 1885), 493.

20. Haughton, *Green Immigrants: The Plants That Transformed America*, 32.

21. Charles F. Wingate, ed., *The Housekeeper: A Journal of Domestic Economy* 2:8 (New York: Howard Lockwood, August 1876), 133.

22. "Sunday School Leaflet of the American Home Missionary Society" (New York: January 1879), 33; Henry Lee, *The Tourist's Guide of Florida and the Winter Resorts of the South* (New York: Charles H. Smith, 1891), 198.

23. William Fawcett, *The Banana: Its Cultivation, Distribution and Commercial Uses* (London: Duckworth, 1913), 243.

24. "Growing Bananas in Florida," *Literary Digest* 79 (October 20, 1923), 76.

25. Bolles, "Commercial Banana Growing" (c. 1924), 1.

26. James H. Collins, "Growing Our Own Bananas: How Florida Is Establishing a New Crop," *Scientific American* 131 (August 1924), 86.

27. Bolles, "Commercial Banana Growing," 3.

28. Collins, "Growing Our Own Bananas: How Florida Is Establishing a New Crop," 86.

29. T. Ralph Robinson, "Banana Growing in Florida," typescript, Bureau of Plant Industry, U.S. Department of Agriculture (July 1, 1925), 3.

30. T. Ralph Robinson, "Banana Growing in Florida," typescript, Bureau of Plant Industry, U.S. Department of Agriculture (January 15, 1934), 3.

31. E. D. Stratton, "Bananas: Fruits, Tropical, N.O.S., Dried or Evaporated Fruits," Association of American Railroads, Railroad Committee for the Study of Transportation, Subcommittee on Economic Study Group 4, typescript (July 24, 1946), foreword, vi.

32. Scott U. Stambaugh, *Bananas in Florida* (Tallahassee: Department of Agriculture, 1952), 4.

33. Stambaugh, *Bananas in Florida*, 73.

34. John F. Mariani, *The Dictionary of American Food and Drink* (New Haven and New York: Ticknor & Fields, 1983), 24.

35. Thomas G. Thrum, comp., *Hawaiian Almanac and Annual for 1891* (Honolulu: Press Publishing, 1890), 27.

36. W. T. Pope, "Banana Culture in Hawaii" 55 (Honolulu: Hawaii Agri-

cultural Experiment Station; Washington, D.C.: Government Printing Office, December 1926), 1.

37. Pope, "Banana Culture in Hawaii," 20.

38. Stratton, "Bananas: Fruits, Tropical, N.O.S., Dried or Evaporated Fruits," 13.

39. Mariani, *The Dictionary of American Food and Drink*, 24.

40. Ned Geeslin, "Success Comes in Bunches for Two Californians," *People* (August 8, 1988), 82; Linda Hollenhorst, "Growin' Bananas," *Organic Gardening* (September 1989), 54–56.

41. S. Annie Frost, *The Godey's Lady's Book Receipts and Household Hints* (Philadelphia: Evans, Stoddart, 1870), 169.

42. Sallie Joy White, *Housekeepers and Home-Makers* (Boston: Jordan, Marsh, 1888), 126.

43. Todd S. Goodholme, ed., *A Domestic Cyclopaedia of Practical Information* (New York: Henry Holt, 1877), 14.

44. S. D. Farrar, *The Homekeeper* (Boston: 1872), 125.

45. Artemis Ward, *The Grocers' Hand-Book and Directory for 1888* (Philadelphia: Philadelphia Grocer Publishing, 1885), 18.

46. William A. Alcott, *The Young House-Keeper* (Boston: George W. Light, 1838).

47. *Visitor's Guide to the Centennial Exhibition and Philadelphia 1876* (Philadelphia: J. B. Lippincott, 1875), 16; *Frank Leslie's Illustrated Historical Register of the Centennial Exposition 1876* 1:7 (New York: Frank Leslie, 1876), 219.

48. *Harper's Weekly* (November 29, 1890), 935.

49. Frederick Upham Adams, *Conquest of the Tropics: The Story of the Creative Enterprises Conducted by United Fruit* (New York: Doubleday, Page, 1914), 21.

50. "Mexican Indians," *Sunday School Advocate* 20:18 (June 22, 1861), 70; "Christmas in Jamaica," *Sunday School Advocate* 33:13 (April 11, 1874), 52; Edward E. Hale, *Sunday School Stories on the Golden Texts of the International Lessons of 1889* (Boston: Roberts Brothers, 1889), 257–68.

51. Charles F. Wingate, ed., *The Housekeeper: A Journal of Domestic Economy* 1:12 (New York: Howard Lockwood, November 1875), 180.

52. Adams, *Conquest of the Tropics*, 23–24.

53. Ruth H. Cloudman, *The Chosen Object: European and American Still Life* (Omaha: Joslyn Art Museum, 1977), iv.

54. William H. Gerdts and Russell Burke, *American Still-Life Painting* (New York: Praeger Publishers, 1971), 175.

55. "Bountiful Board," American painting 1840–1860, in the Abby Aldrich Rockefeller Folk Art Collection, plate 38; *Four Centuries of Still Life* (Allentown Art Museum Catalog, December 12, 1959–January 31, 1960); "Dessert," Morston Constantine Ream (1840–1898), Plate 40, *American Still Lifes of the Nineteenth Century* (New York: Hirschl and Adler Galleries, December 1971); "Fruit and Asparagus," William Michael Harnett, 1875, Plate 46, *American Cornucopia: 19th Century Still Lifes and Studies* (Pittsburgh: Carnegie-Mellon University, Hunt Institute for Botanical Documentation, 1976).

56. Katharine Morrison McClinton, "The Dining Room Picture," *Spinning Wheel* 34:3 (April 1978), 25.

57. *Prang's Chromo* (Boston: April, 1868), 4; *L. Prang & Co.'s Catalogue for Fall, 1878* (Boston: L. Prang, 1878), 7; *J. Jay Gould's Catalogue of Chromos, Engravings, Album Gems, Lithographs, Picture Frames, Picture Books* (Boston: n.d.); *Globe Printing House Catalogue: Carter's Oil Chromos, Carter's Popular Crayons* 8 (East Hampstead, New Hampshire: 1877).

58. *Ladies' Manual of Art* (Philadelphia: American Mutual Library Association, 1887), 151.

59. "Table Garniture," *The Cook* 1:15 (July 6, 1885), 7.

60. Maria Parloa, *Miss Parloa's Kitchen Companion* (Boston: Estes and Lauriat, 1887), 697.

61. S. D. Power, *Anna Maria's Housekeeping* (Boston: D. Lothrop, 1884), 41.

62. *The Cook: A Weekly Handbook of Domestic Culinary Art for All Housekeepers* 1:10 (June 1, 1885), 3.

63. *The Cook: A Weekly Handbook of Domestic Culinary Art For All Housekeepers* 1:11 (June 8, 1885), 12.

64. Brownlea, "The Best Banana Bred," 22.

65. "The Banana as the Basis of a New Industry," *Scientific American* 80 (March 4, 1899), 137.

66. Mel T. Cook, "The Banana," *Scientific American Supplement* 60 (September 23, 1905), 24847.

2. POLITICS AND BANANAS

1. Thomas L. Karnes, *Tropical Enterprise: The Standard Fruit and Steamship Company in Latin America* (Baton Rouge: Louisiana State University Press, 1978), 4.

2. "Some Facts about Bananas," *Scientific American* 75, (October 10, 1896), 284.

3. "The Banana," *Harper's Weekly* 40 (July 25, 1896), 734.

4. "The Banana as the Basis of a New Industry," *Scientific American* 80 (March 4, 1899), 137.

5. Leslie Bethell, ed., *Central America since Independence* (New York: Cambridge University Press, 1991), 54.

6. Bethell, ed., *Central America since Independence*, 51.

7. Bethell, ed., *Central America since Independence*, 54.

8. Marina Warner, *No Go the Bogeyman: Scaring, Lulling, and Making Mock* (New York: Farrar, Straus and Giroux, 1998), 357; "Yes, They Sell More Bananas," *Business Week* (July 8, 1967), 94.

9. Philip Keep Reynolds, *The Banana: Its History, Cultivation, and Place among Staple Foods* (Boston: Houghton Mifflin, 1927), 154.

10. Bethell, ed., *Central America since Independence*, 52.

11. Middle America Information Bureau, "Middle America and Bananas" (New York: United Fruit), 1946/47, 7.

12. Karnes, *Tropical Enterprise*, 11.

13. Karnes, *Tropical Enterprise*, 10–11.

14. Karnes, *Tropical Enterprise*, 29.

15. Bethell, ed., *Central America since Independence*, 54.

16. Bethell, ed., *Central America since Independence*, 51.

17. Karnes, *Tropical Enterprise*, xi.

18. Karnes, *Tropical Enterprise*, 291.

19. Karnes, *Tropical Enterprise*, 294.

20. Henry F. Pringle, "A Jonah Who Swallowed the Whale: S. Zemurray," *American Magazine* 116 (September 1933), 114.

21. Bethell, ed. *Central America since Independence*, 51.

22. Pringle, "A Jonah Who Swallowed the Whale: S. Zemurray," 45; Karnes, *Tropical Enterprise*, 178.

23. Karnes, *Tropical Enterprise*, 178.

24. Karnes, *Tropical Enterprise*, 52.

25. *New York Times* (July 1, 1913), 11.

26. *New York Times* (July 2, 1913), 8.

27. *New York Times* (July 12, 1913), 3.

28. *New York Times* (July 12, 1913), 3.

29. *New York Times* (July 12, 1913), 6.

30. *New York Times* (July 23, 1913), 7.

31. *New York Times* (July 30, 1913), 6.

32. *New York Times* (August 28, 1913), 10.

33. *New York Times* (September 11, 1913), 5.

34. *New York Times* (September 17, 1913), 8.
35. Frederick Upham Adams, *Conquest of the Tropics: The Story of the Creative Enterprises Conducted by United Fruit* (New York: Doubleday, Page, 1914), 342.
36. Karnes, *Tropical Enterprise,* 57.
37. "20,000 Bunches Bananas Brought from Colombia," *Boston Globe* (July 15, 1918), 12.
38. "First Jamaican Bananas in Months," *Boston Globe* (November 9, 1918), 6.
39. Cartoon, *Boston Globe* (July 16, 1998), 6.
40. Beverly Thomas Galloway, "Suggestions and Comments on Banana Growing and Some Related Subjects" (typescript, July 6, 1927).
41. "United Fruit: 50,000,000 Bunches Boost 1935 Profits," *Newsweek* 5 (March 30, 1935), 34.
42. "United Fruit: 50,000,000 Bunches Boost 1935 Profits," 34.
43. "Bananas Are Back," *Time* (March 18, 1946), 38.
44. "Bananas Are Back," 40.
45. Karnes, *Tropical Enterprise,* 207
46. E. D. Stratton, "Bananas: Fruits, Tropical, N.O.S., Dried or Evaporated Fruits," Association of American Railroads, Railroad Committee for the Study of Transportation, Subcommittee on Economic Study Group 4, typescript (July 24, 1946), 13.
47. Stratton, "Bananas: Fruits, Tropical, N.O.S., Dried or Evaporated Fruits," 13.
48. Karnes, *Tropical Enterprise,* 247.
49. John H. Melville, *The Great White Fleet* (New York: Vantage Press, 1976), 179.
50. "Bananas Are Back," 38.
51. Stratton, "Bananas: Fruits, Tropical, N.O.S., Dried or Evaporated Fruits," v.
52. Karnes, *Tropical Enterprise,* 210; Bethell, ed., *Central America since Independence,* 199.
53. Karnes, *Tropical Enterprise,* 144.
54. Karnes, *Tropical Enterprise,* 165.
55. Philippe Bourgois, *Ethnicity at Work: Divided Labor on a Central American Banana Plantation* (Baltimore: Johns Hopkins University Press, 1989), 16.
56. Charles Morrow Wilson, "Green Dragon of the Tropics," *Scientific American* 162 (April 1940), 199.

57. Karnes, *Tropical Enterprise*, 180.

58. George C. Compton, "The Banana Business," *Americas* 8 (July 1956), 33; Wilson, "Green Dragon of the Tropics," 200.

59. Karnes, *Tropical Enterprise*, 80; "United Fruit: 50,000,000 Bunches Boost 1935 Profits," 36.

60. E-mail communication from Steve Marquardt, University of Washington (December 12, 1997).

61. Eleanor Lothrop, "Banana from Ground to Grocer," *Natural History* 65 (November 1956) 463; Wilson, "Green Dragon of the Tropics," 201.

62. Karnes, *Tropical Enterprise*, 187.

63. Tom Gill, "You've Got To Go after It: Trip in Search of Facts about Central America's Banana Industry," *American Magazine* 128 (September 1939), 90; Wilson, "Green Dragon of the Tropics," 201.

64. "Engineering Better Bananas," *Popular Science* (August 1946), 112; "Bananas Are Back," 40.

65. Philip T. Leonard, "Banana Highball," *Travel* (March 1949), 26.

66. Lothrop, "Banana from Ground to Grocer," 501; Leonard, "Banana Highball," 27.

67. R. H. Stover and N. W. Simmonds, *Bananas* (New York: Longman Scientific and Technical, 1987), 423.

68. Donald R. Strong, "Banana's Best Friend," *Natural History* 93 (December 1984), 55–56.

69. Shannon Brownlea, "The Best Banana Bred," *Atlantic* 264 (September 1989), 24; Eleena De Lisser, "Bananas You Love on Your Cornflakes Are in Some Danger," *Wall Street Journal* (April 10, 1995), 1.

70. Karnes, *Tropical Enterprise*, 68; R. E. B. McKenney, "Central American Banana Blight," *Science* 31 (May 13, 1910), 750; Bethell, ed., *Central America since Independence*, 53.

71. Bethell, ed., *Central America since Independence*, 53.

72. Bethell, ed., *Central America since Independence*, 90.

73. Stover and Simmonds, *Bananas*, 426.

74. Stover and Simmonds, *Bananas*, 423, 426.

75. Stover and Simmonds, *Bananas*, 426.

76. Stover and Simmonds, *Bananas*, 424, 425.

78. De Lisser, "Bananas You Love on Your Cornflakes Are in Some Danger," 1.

79. Brownlea, "The Best Banana Bred," 24.

80. "Can a Banana Splice Save the Banana Split?" *Discover* 8 (August 1987), 7.

81. De Lisser, "Bananas You Love on Your Cornflakes Are in Some Danger," 1.

82. De Lisser, "Bananas You Love on Your Cornflakes Are in Some Danger," 13.

83. *Mother Jones* (June 1989), 22–27.

84. Carole Sugarman, "Small Amount of Tainted Bananas Found," *Washington Post* (June 5, 1991), A14; Maura Dolan, "Bananas To Be Monitored for Pesticide Level," *Los Angeles Times* (June 13, 1991), A1.

85. "Living on Earth," National Public Radio, August 1992.

86. "Better Bananas," *Maine Organic Farmer and Gardener* (March/April 1993), 7.

87. Stover and Simmonds, *Bananas*, 431.

88. Stover and Simmonds, *Bananas*, 430.

89. Stover and Simmonds, *Bananas*, 431.

90. Stover and Simmonds, *Bananas*, 425.

91. Lisa Mirabile, ed., *International Directory of Company Histories* 2 (Chicago: St. James Press, 1990), 596.

92. Mirabile, ed., *International Directory of Company Histories*, 596.

93. Mirabile, ed., *International Directory of Company Histories*, 596.

94. Mirabile, ed., *International Directory of Company Histories*, 596.

95. William Braznell, *California's Finest: The History of Del Monte Corporation and the Del Monte Brand* (Del Monte Corporation, 1982), 160.

96. Thomas Bancroft, "A New Kind of Cash Cow," *Forbes* (October 14, 1991), 52.

97. Bancroft, "A New Kind of Cash Cow," 54.

98. Bancroft, "A New Kind of Cash Cow," 52.

99. Bancroft, "A New Kind of Cash Cow," 52.

100. "Bitter Truth Behind Bananas," *TransAfrica Forum Update* (November–December 1996).

101. Nora Boustany, "Yes, We Have No Banana Pact," *Washington Post* (November 20, 1998), A50.

102. Nora Boustany, "Yes, We Have No Banana Pact," A50.

103. Michael A. Samuels, "Beef Wars," *Washington Post* (July 13, 1999), A19.

104. http://enquirer.com/chiquita/news.html (May 29, 1998).

105. John Ward Anderson, "Mitch Left Honduras a Republic without Bananas," *Washington Post* (November 19, 1988), A39.

106. John Ward Anderson, "Tropical Storm Mitch Uprooted Crops, Lives," *Washington Post* (November 19, 1998), A40.

3. TRANSPORTING BANANAS

1. "Three Thousand Million Bananas a Year," *Review of Reviews, American* 44 (July 1911), 99; John F. Mariani, *The Dictionary of American Food and Drink* (New Haven and New York: Ticknor & Fields, 1983), 24; Waverly Root and Richard deRochemont, *Eating in America: A History* (New York: Morrow, 1976), 154.

2. Mariani, *The Dictionary of American Food and Drink,* 24.

3. Root and deRochemont, *Eating in America: A History,* 154.

4. *Bananas* (Washington, D.C.: Pan American Union, 1956), 5.

5. B. Roueche, "The Humblest Fruit," *New Yorker* 49 (October 1, 1973), 43.

6. *Bananas,* 5.

7. Janet McKenzie Hill, ed., *A Short History of the Banana and a Few Recipes for Its Use* (United Fruit, 1904), 4.

8. Thomas L. Karnes, *Tropical Enterprise: The Standard Fruit and Steamship Company in Latin America* (Baton Rouge: Louisiana State University Press, 1978), 9, 11.

9. Roueche, "The Humblest Fruit," 43.

10. Hill, ed. *A Short History of the Banana and a Few Recipes for Its Use,* 7.

11. "Reply of United Fruit to Statement Addressed to the Committee on Interstate Commerce of the United States Senate by Everett Wheeler and John W. Griffin of Counsel for American Banana Company" (c. 1908), 3.

12. "Reply of United Fruit to Statement," 11.

13. Thomas Ewing Dabney, "Mechanical Stevedore That Handles Bananas," *Scientific American* 123 (November 27, 1920), 558.

14. "Unloading Bananas by Machinery," *Scientific American Supplement* 79 (April 3, 1915), 209.

15. Karnes, *Tropical Enterprise,* 30.

16. "Unloading Bananas by Machinery," 209.

17. Dabney, "Mechanical Stevedore That Handles Bananas," 549.

18. Education Department, *The Story of the Banana,* 39.

19. Karnes, *Tropical Enterprise,* 9.

20. Karnes, *Tropical Enterprise,* 7.

21. Karnes, *Tropical Enterprise,* 7; *United Fruit* (Boston: Edgerly and Crocker, 1902), 5.

22. Grace Agnes Thompson, "The Story of a Great New England Enterprise," *New England Magazine* 53 (May 1915), 12.

23. Hill, ed., *A Short History of the Banana and a Few Recipes for Its Use*, 6.

24. Roueche, "The Humblest Fruit," 44.

25. Hill, ed., *A Short History of the Banana and a Few Recipes for Its Use*, 89.

26. Alfred D. Chandler, Jr., *The Visible Hand: The Managerial Revolution in American Business* (Cambridge: Belknap Press of Harvard University Press, 1977), 346.

27. "United Fruit: 50,000,000 Bunches Boost 1935 Profits," *Newsweek* 5 (March 30, 1935), 35.

28. *United Fruit*, 2.

29. Hill, *A Short History of the Banana and a Few Recipes for Its Use*, 31.

30. Julius Chambers, *A Happy Month in Jamaica*, United Fruit's Steamship Lines (c. 1915), no page numbers.

31. "Great White Fleet," *Pan-American Magazine* (December 1918), inside front cover.

32. William McFee, *The Gates of the Caribbean: The Story of a Great White Fleet Caribbean Cruise* (United Fruit Steamship Service, 1922), 24.

33. *General Instructions for the Information and Guidance of All Employees* (Boston: United Fruit, 1929), 81.

34. Karnes, *Tropical Enterprise*, 170.

35. Karnes, *Tropical Enterprise*, 191.

36. United Fruit advertisement, *Fortune* (March 1933), 10.

37. Bananas Are Back," *Time* (March 18, 1946), 38.

38. *UF Report* 4, 1954, 27.

39. George A. Peltz, ed., *The Housewife's Library* (Philadelphia, New York, Boston, Cincinnati, Chicago, St. Louis, Kansas City: Hubbard Brothers, 1883), 201.

40. *The Cook: A Weekly Handbook of Domestic Culinary Art for All Housekeepers* 1:12 (June 15, 1885), 8.

41. Marion Harland, *Breakfast, Dinner and Supper: How To Cook and How To Serve Them* (New York: George J. McLeod, 1897), 201.

42. Karnes, *Tropical Enterprise*, 20.

43. "The Banana," *Harper's Weekly* 40 (July 25, 1896), 734.

44. "United Fruit: 50,000,000 Bunches Boost 1935 Profits," 35.

45. Karnes, *Tropical Enterprise*, 28.

46. "Fruit Dispatch Company 1898–1923," *Fruit Dispatch* 9:8 (December 1923), 369.

47. "Three Thousand Million Bananas a Year," *Review of Reviews, American* 44 (July 1911), 102.

48. "Fruit Dispatch Company 1898–1923," 370.

49. E. D. Stratton, "Bananas: Fruits, Tropical, N.O.S., Dried or Evapo-

rated Fruits," Association of American Railroads, Railroad Committee for the Study of Transportation, Subcommittee on Economic Study Group 4, typescript (July 24, 1946), x.

50. Philip Keep Reynolds, *The Banana: Its History, Cultivation and Place among Staple Foods* (Boston: Houghton Mifflin, 1927), 96.

51. "Fruit Dispatch Company 1898–1923," 370.

52. Education Department, *The Story of the Banana*, 40.

53. Karnes, *Tropical Enterprise*, 51.

54. Education Department, *The Story of the Banana*, 41.

55. Reynolds, *The Banana: Its History, Cultivation and Place among Staple Foods*, 95.

56. G. Harold Powell, "The Handling of Fruit for Transportation," Year Book (U.S. Department of Agriculture, 1905), 359.

57. Karnes, *Tropical Enterprise*, 8.

58. Karnes, *Tropical Enterprise*, 25.

59. Karnes, *Tropical Enterprise*, 25.

60. Karnes, *Tropical Enterprise*, 165.

61. Education Department, *The Story of the Banana*, 41.

62. William R. Childs, *Trucking and the Public Interest* (Knoxville: University of Tennessee Press, 1985),19.

63. Mary Beth Norton, et al., *A People and a Nation* (Boston: Houghton Mifflin, 1986), 745.

64. Childs, *Trucking and the Public Interest*, 20.

65. "Top Banana," *Fortune* (May 1953), 166.

66. Childs, *Trucking and the Public Interest*, 21.

4 · SELLING BANANAS

1. Frederick Upham Adams, *Conquest of the Tropics: The Story of the Creative Enterprises Conducted by United Fruit* (New York: Doubleday, Page, 1914), 75.

2. Adams, *Conquest of the Tropics*, 73.

3. "Unloading a Banana Steamer," *Harper's Weekly* 38 (April 21, 1894), 366.

4. "The Banana," *Harper's Weekly* 40 (July 25, 1896), 734.

5. "Unloading a Banana Steamer," 366.

6. "Unloading a Banana Steamer," 366.

7. Artemis Ward, *The Grocers' Hand-Book and Directory for 1886* (Philadelphia: Philadelphia Grocer Publishing, 1885), 18.

8. "Fruit Dispatch Company 1898–1923," *Fruit Dispatch* 9:8 (December 1923), 301.

9. G. Harold Powell, "The Handling of Fruit for Transportation," *Year Book* (U.S. Department of Agriculture, 1905), 349.

10. *United Fruit* (Boston: Edgerly and Crocker, 1902), 5.

11. "Fruit Dispatch Company 1898–1923," 362.

12. "United Fruit: 50,000,000 Bunches Boost 1935 Profits," *Newsweek* 5 (March 30, 1935), 35.

13. Eleanor Lothrop, "Banana from Ground to Grocer," *Natural History* 65 (November 1956), 503.

14. Equipment Department, *Banana Ripening Manual,* Circular 14 (New York: Fruit Dispatch Company, 1933), 9.

15. Stephanie Witt Sedgwick, "Yes! We Have Nice Bananas," *Washington Post* (February 3, 1999), F1.

16. Philip K. Reynolds, *The Story of the Banana* (Washington, D.C.: Government Printing Office, 1923), 26.

17. Education Department, *The Story of the Banana* (Boston: United Fruit, 1936), 44.

18. Philip Keep Reynolds, *The Banana: Its History, Cultivation and Place among Staple Foods* (Boston: Houghton Mifflin, 1927), 98.

19. *The Story of the Banana* (3d rev. ed., Boston: United Fruit, 1925), 42.

20. Personal communication, Ann Lovell, curator of the Banana Museum, Auburn, Washington, August 1995.

21. E. D. Stratton, "Bananas: Fruits, Tropical, N.O.S., Dried or Evaporated Fruits," Association of American Railroads, Railroad Committee for the Study of Transportation, Subcommittee on Economic Study group 4, typescript (July 24, 1946), 27.

22. Hugh M. Smith, Wendell E. Clement, William S. Hoofnagle, "Merchandising of Selected Food Items in Grocery Stores," Marketing Research Report 111, Agricultural Marketing Service (U.S. Department of Agriculture, Washington, D.C., February 1956), 2.

23. Paul Franklin Shaffer, "Produce Packaging at the Central Warehouse—Bananas," Agricultural Research Service, New Series ARS 52-7 (U.S. Department of Agriculture, October 1965), 3.

24. Thomas L. Karnes, *Tropical Enterprise: Standard Fruit and Steamship Company in Latin America* (Baton Rouge: Louisiana State University Press, 1978), 183.

25. "Methods, Equipment, and Facilities for Receiving, Ripening, and Packing Bananas," Marketing Research Report 92, Agricultural Mar-

keting Service (U.S. Department of Agriculture, Washington, D.C., June 1955), 1.

26. Chiquita advertisement, *Restaurants & Institutions* (April 3, 1991), 153.

27. Dole advertisement, *Restaurants & Institutions* (April 3, 1991), 147.

28. Karnes, *Tropical Enterprise,* 284.

29. Karnes, *Tropical Enterprise,* 287.

30. R. H. Stover and N. W. Simmonds, *Bananas* (New York: Longman Scientific and Technical, 1987), 423.

31. Karnes, *Tropical Enterprise,* 285.

32. Laura Shapiro, *Perfection Salad: Women and Cooking at the Turn of the Century* (New York: Farrar, Straus and Giroux, 1986), 231.

33. "Fruit Dispatch Company 1898–1923," 365.

34. "Scientific Market Research Brief for Fruit Dispatch Company" (December 1929, typescript, no page numbers).

35. Proof of 1930 Advertising, Exhibit B, Scientific Market Research Brief for Fruit Dispatch Company (December 1929, typescript, no page numbers).

36. "Chiquita Goes to School," *U.F. Report* 2 (1954), 1.

37. Home Economics Department, *A Study of the Banana: Its Every-Day Use and Food Value* (New York: United Fruit, 1939), 4.

38. Classroom in Sublette, Kansas, April 1941, photograph by Irving Rusinow for the Bureau of Agricultural Economics, Division of Economic Information, Community Studies Photographs, RG 83-G, Still Picture Branch, National Archives, College Park, Maryland.

39. "Chiquita Goes to School," 2.

40. *Unifruitco* 21:3 (United Fruit, June/July 1962), 2.

41. *Unifruitco,* 2.

42. *Unifruitco* 27:1 (United Fruit, January 31, 1969, 7).

43. *Unifruitco* 25:10 (United Fruit, October 31, 1967), 7.

44. Sara Olkon, "Wanted: A Person Who Can Sing While Wearing a Bowl of Fruit," *Wall Street Journal* (May 4, 1994), B1.

45. Laura Bird, "Chiquita's Ad Archive: The Picture of Health," *Adweek's Marketing Week* (January 7, 1991), 32.

46. Warren Dotz, *Advertising Character Collectibles* (Paducah, Kentucky: Collector Books, 1993), 34.

47. Olkon, "Wanted: A Person Who Can Sing While Wearing a Bowl of Fruit," B1; David Widner, "America's Going Bananas," *Reader's Digest* (July 1986), 118.

48. *U.F. Report* 2 (1954), 3.

49. Anna May Wilson, "Forbidden Fruit?" *Today's Health* (May 1951), 51.

50. "Bananas, Always in Season," *Southern Living* (March 1983), 226.

51. *Unifruitco* 21:3, 4.

52. "Yes, They Sell More Bananas," *Business Week* (July 8, 1967), 92.

53. Stover and Simmonds, *Bananas,* 427.

54. *Sales Newsletter* 3:1 (Boston: United Fruit Sales Corporation, January 1964), 2.

55. *Unifruitco* 23:7, 3.

56. *Unifruitco* 24:1, 1.

57. *Unifruitco* 24:5, 7.

58. *Unifruitco* 24:9, 2, 3; *The Workbasket* 17:4 (January 1952), 73.

59. Bird, "Chiquita's Ad Archive: The Picture of Health," 33.

60. "Chiquita's Ad Archive: The Picture of Health," 33.

61. *New York Times* (July 8, 1992), D1.

62. Olkon, "Wanted: A Person Who Can Sing While Wearing a Bowl of Fruit," B1.

63. *Unifruitco* 24:10, 1.

64. Chiquita Brand Bananas, *Parents Magazine* (September 1967), 52.

65. *Unifruitco* 23:7, 1.

66. *Unifruitco* 23:15, 6.

67. "The Great Outdoors Offer from Chiquita," *Ebony* (July 1977), 135.

68. Bird, "Chiquita's Ad Archive: The Picture of Health," 32.

69. Bird, "Chiquita's Ad Archive: The Picture of Health," 33.

70. Bird, "Chiquita's Ad Archive: The Picture of Health," 32.

71. Fara Warner, "Surprise! Chiquita Advises: Eat Bananas," *Adweek's Marketing Week* (April 29, 1991), 8.

72. *New York Times* (August 22, 1992), 35.

73. "Marketing Turns Castoff into Top Lunch Bananas," *New York Times* (August 22, 1992), 35L.

74. James B. Twitchell, *AdCult USA: The Triumph of Advertising in American Culture* (New York: Columbia University Press), 1996.

5. PERIL AND PANACEA

1. E. B. Duffey, *The Ladies' and Gentlemen's Etiquette: A Complete Manual of the Manners and Dress of American Society* (Philadelphia: Porter and Coates, 1877), 144.

2. George A. Peltz, ed., *The Housewife's Library* (Philadelphia, New York,

Boston, Cincinnati, Chicago, St. Louis, and Kansas City: Hubbard Brothers, 1883), 201.

3. Maria Parloa, *Home Economics* (New York: The Century, 1898, 227.

4. Maria Parloa, *First Principles of Household Management and Cookery* (Boston: Houghton Mifflin, 1882), 45.

5. (Mrs.) D. A. Lincoln, *Mrs Lincoln's Boston Cook Book* (Boston: Roberts Brothers, 1888), 391.

6. Catherine Owen, "Cheap Living in Cities," *The Home-Maker* 2:2 (May 1889), 126.

7. Sidney W. Mintz, *Sweetness and Power: the Place of Sugar in Modern History* (New York: Viking Press, 1985), 76.

8. Joseph B. Lyman and Laura E. Lyman, *The Philosophy of House-Keeping* (Hartford: Goodwin and Betts, 1867), 304.

9. (Mrs.) S. T. Rorer, *Good Cooking* (Philadelphia: Curtis Publishing, 1898), 213.

10. "Our Baby In June," *Housekeeper's Weekly* (June 4, 1892), 8.

11. "To the Police Force," *The Cook* 1:13 (June 22, 1885), 4.

12. Mary Ellen Chase, *A Goodly Heritage* (New York: Henry Holt, 1932), 167–68.

13. "Bananas as Food," *Marylander and Herald* (Princess Anne, Maryland, January 25, 1916).

14. "Cook Your Bananas," *Literary Digest* 56 (February 16, 1918), 22.

15. "What Do You Know about It?" *Ladies Home Journal* 45 (March 1928), 48.

16. Samuel C. Prescott, "Consider The Banana," *Good Housekeeping* 65 (October 1917), 79.

17. "What Do You Know about It?" *Ladies Home Journal,* 48.

18. Mary Corbin Sies, "The Domestic Mission of the Privileged American Suburban Homemaker, 1877–1917: A Reassessment" in *Making The American Home: Middle-Class Women and Domestic Material Culture 1840–1940,* ed. Marilyn Ferris Motz and Pat Browne (Bowling Green, Ohio: Bowling Green State University/Popular Press, 1988), 196.

19. Laura Shapiro, *Perfection Salad: Women and Cooking at the Turn of the Century* (New York: Farrar, Straus and Giroux, 1986), 5.

20. Glenna Matthews, *"Just a Housewife:" The Rise and Fall of Domesticity in America* (New York: Oxford University Press, 1987), 149.

21. Ann Hertzler, "Food and Nutrition: Integrative Themes and Content," *Definitive Themes in Home Economics and Their Impact on Families*

1909–1984 (Washington, D.C.: American Home Economics Association, 1984), 73.

22. Phyllis Palmer, *Domesticity and Dirt: Housewives and Domestic Servants in the United States, 1920–1945* (Philadelphia: Temple University Press, 1989), 53.

23. Kenneth L. Burden and Robert Williams, *Microbiology* (New York: Macmillan, 1964), 38.

24. Isaac Asimov, *How Did We Find Out about Vitamins?* (New York: Walker, 1974), 15.

25. H. W. Conn, *Bacteria, Yeasts, and Molds in the Home* (3d rev. ed., Boston: Ginn, 1932), v.

26. Winifred Wishard, "Bananas, The Mainstay of the Menu," *Pictorial Review* 28 (April 1927), 39.

27. "Cook Your Bananas," 22.

28. Prescott, "Consider the Banana," 79.

29. "What Do You Know about It?" 48.

30. "The Banana—A Fruit in a Sterile Package," *Journal of the American Medical Association* 60 (January 18, 1913), 209.

31. Skinner, Sherman, and Esselen, *The Food Value of the Banana* (Boston: W. M. Leonard, 1926), 8.

32. "Food Prejudices and Food Facts," *The Journal of the American Medical Association* 89 (November 5, 1927), 1608.

33. "What Do You Know about It?" 48.

34. Victor C. Myers and Anton R. Rose, "Report on the Food Value of the Banana," *Journal of the American Medical Association* (Chicago, April 7, 1917), 1022.

35. Education Department, *The Story of the Banana* (5th ed., Boston: United Fruit, 1929), 37.

36. Mintz, *Sweetness and Power,* 134.

37. Skinner, Sherman, and Esselen, *The Food Value of the Banana,* 17.

38. "The Nutritive Value of the Banana," *Journal of the American Medical Association* 71 (December 28, 1918), 2158.

39. Asimov, *How Did We Find Out about Vitamins?* 31.

40. Walter H. Eddy and Minerva Kellogg, "The Place of The Banana in the Diet," *American Journal of Public Health* 17 (January 1927), 31.

41. "What Do You Know about It?" 48.

42. Nell B. Nichols, "Bananas for the Underweight," *Parents Magazine* 5 (October 1930), 38.

43. Committee on Foods, "United Fruit Advertising Campaign for Ba-

nanas," *Journal of the American Medical Association* 97 (December 19, 1931), 1890.

44. Lotta Jean Bogert, *Dietary Uses of the Banana in Health and Disease* (New York: United Fruit, 1935), 32.

45. Burdon and Williams, *Microbiology*, 615.

46. Michael E. Teller, *The Tuberculosis Movement: A Public Health Campaign in the Progressive Era* (New York: Greenwood Press, 1988), 1.

47. Teller, *The Tuberculosis Movement: A Public Health Campaign in the Progressive Era*, 43.

48. Hilbert F. Day, "Sunshine Camp in Cambridge," *Journal of the National Education Association* 57 (June 1928), 169.

49. Lotta Jean Bogert, *Dietary Uses of the Banana in Health and Disease* (New York: United Fruit, 1935), 32.

50. Day, "Sunshine Camp in Cambridge," 250.

51. Education Department, *The Story of the Banana*, 38. 52. 52. Albert W. Fellows, "The Summer Day Camp of Bangor," *Maine Medical Journal* 26 (1935), 18.

53. John J. McNamara, "Lowell Fights Undernourishment among Its School Children," *American Journal of Public Health* 19 (1929), 605.

54. J. Cyril Eby, "Malnutrition," *Southern Medical Journal* 23 (1930), 842.

55. Frank Ryan, *The Forgotten Plague: How the Battle Against Tuberculosis Was Won—and Lost* (Boston: Little, Brown, 1992), 28.

56. Ryan, *The Forgotten Plague*, xvi.

57. "Bananas Are Good for Children," *Hygeia* 17 (October 1939), 960.

58. *Ladies Home Journal* (April 1976), 127.

59. United Fruit Research Department, *Nutritive and Therapeutic Values of the Banana: A Digest of Scientific Literature* (Boston: G. H. Company, 1936), 25.

60. "What Do You Know about It?" 48.

61. Victor C. Myers and Anton R. Rose, "Report on the Food Value of the Banana," *Journal of the American Medical Association* (Chicago: April 7, 1917), 1024.

62. *Nutritive and Therapeutic Values of the Banana: A Digest of Scientific Literature* (Boston: United Fruit Research Department, 1936), 5.

63. "Banana—Cure for Childhood Disease," *Literary Digest* 113 (June 25, 1932), 24.

64. Robert Berkow, ed., *Merck Manual of Diagnosis and Therapy* (Rahway: Merck Sharp & Dohme Research Laboratories, 1982), 775.

65. "Bananas Are Essential to Diet in Celiac Disease," *Hygeia: The Health Magazine* 10 (September 1932), 854.

66. "Banana Priorities," *Newsweek* 20 (August 10, 1942), 57.

67. Lotta Jean Bogert, *Dietary Uses of the Banana in Health and Disease* (New York: United Fruit, 1935), 32.

68. "Banana Priorities," 57.

69. "Banana Priorities," 57.

70. "Banana Priorities," 57.

71. "Yes, We Have No Bananas, But Babies Need Not Suffer," *Science Newsletter* 42 (August 8, 1942), 87.

72. Jane Nickerson, "Bananas—Cooked," *New York Times Magazine* (September 14, 1947), 42.

73. "Antibiotic from Bananas," *Science Newsletter* 55 (April 23, 1949), 260.

74. T. Philip Waalkes et al., "Serotonin, Norepinephrine, and Related Compounds in Bananas," *Science* 127 (March 21, 1958), 649.

75. "Chemicals in Bananas," *Science Newsletter* 73 (April 5, 1958), 215.

76. Carol Keough, "The Beautiful Banana," *Organic Gardening* 26 (January 1979), 139.

77. Rick Weiss, "Vaccine A-Peel: Researchers Aim at a Disease-Preventing Banana," *Washington Post* (April 11, 1995), Health Section, 7.

78. Rick Weiss, "Replacing Needles with Nibbles to Put the Bite on Disease," *Washington Post* (May 4, 1998), A3.

79. George A. Harrop, "A Milk and Banana Diet for the Treatment of Obesity," *Journal of the American Medical Association* 102 (1934), 2003.

80. *House Beautiful* (October 1977), 120.

81. "Sweet Treat: Bananas," *Good Housekeeping* 194 (March 1982), 178.

82. *Star-Ledger* (Newark, New Jersey, May 12, 1993), 27.

83. "How Many Bananas in a Marathon?" *Washington Post* (October 21, 1995), B9.

84. "Back Country Banana," *Sierra* (March/April 1995), 27.

85. *Title Nine Sports Catalog* (Spring/Summer 1993), 2.

86. *Boston Sunday Globe* (October 6, 1918), 30.

87. Ann Landers, "More on the Wizardry of Wart Removal," *New Haven Register* (June 14, 1993), 17.

88. Ann Landers, *Washington Post* (September 21, 1997).

89. Ann Landers, *Washington Post* (November 30, 1997).

6. EATING BANANAS

1. Charles F. Wingate, ed., *The Housekeeper: A Journal of Domestic Economy* 11:6 (June 1876), 93.

2. Marion Harland, *House and Home: A Complete Housewife's Guide* (Philadelphia: W. Ziegler, 1889), 505.

3. "A Christmas Dinner," *The Ladies' World* (December, 1896), 8.

4. *The Home-Maker* (November 1888), 127.

5. Menu, Winterthur Manuscript Collection.

6. Menu collection, Winterthur Museum and Library, Rare Book Room.

7. *Good Housekeeping* (August 30, 1890), ii.

8. Walter R. Houghton, James K. Beck, James A. Woodburn, Horace R. Hoffman, A. B. Philputt, A. E. Davis, (Mrs.) W. R. Houghton, *American Etiquette and Rules of Politeness* (Indianapolis: A. E. Davis Publisher, 1882), 171.; Maud C. Cooke, *Our Social Manual for All Occasions or Approved Etiquette of To-Day* (Chicago and Philadelphia: Monarch Book Company, 1896), 226.

9. Florence Marion Hall, *The Correct Thing in Good Society* (Boston: Estes and Lauriat, 1888), 101.

10. *175 Choice Recipes Mainly Furnished by Members of the Chicago Women's Club* (Chicago: Charles H. Keer, 1887), 4.

11. *Good Housekeeping* (July 23, 1887), ii.

12. Filippini, *One Hundred Desserts* (New York: H. M. Caldwell, 1893).

13. Horace R. Allen, *The American Home and Farm Cyclopedia* (Philadelphia: Thompson Publishing, 1890), 487.

14. Theodore Francis Garrett, ed., *Encyclopedia of Practical Cookery* (Philadelphia: Hudson Importing, 1893), 70.

15. "Bananas as Food," *Marylander and Herald* (Princess Anne, Maryland, January 25, 1916).

16. *American Domestic Cyclopaedia* (New York: F. M. Lupton, 1890), 306.

17. *Delicate Dishes: A Cook Book Compiled by Ladies of St. Paul's Church* (Chicago, 1896), 82.

18. "A Spring-Time Breakfast," *Housekeeper's Weekly* 3:19 (May 7, 1892), 14.

19. "Puffed Wheat or Rice with Bananas," *Woman's Home Companion* (March 1910), 58.

20. "Puffed Wheat and Puffed Rice," *Ladies Home Journal* (February 1918), 54.

21. "Shredded Ralston," *American Magazine* (November 1939), 143.

22. William A. Murrill, "The Banana and Its Uses: Getting Acquainted with This Tropical Fruit of Which There Are over Seventy Varieties," *Scientific American* 125a (December 1921), 119.

23. "From the Tropics to Your Table" (New York: Fruit Dispatch Company, 1926), 28.

24. David Widner, "America's Going Bananas," *Reader's Digest* 129 (July 1986), 116.

25. Janet McKenzie Hill, ed., *A Short History of the Banana and a Few Recipes for Its Use* (Boston: United Fruit), 1904.

26. Harland, *House and Home: A Complete Cook-Book and Housewife's Guide*, 387.

27. "Unloading a Banana Steamer," *Harper's Weekly* 38 (April 21, 1894), 366–67.

28. Sidney Mintz, *Sweetness and Power: The Place of Sugar in Modern History* (New York: Elizabeth Seaton Books/Viking), 1985.

29. B. W. Bryant, *A Bill of Fare for Everyday in the Year* (October 1–14, 1892).

30. *Chicago Record Cook Book: Seasonable, Inexpensive Bills of Fare for Every Day in the Year* (Chicago: Chicago Record, 1896), 428.

31. Francis X. Clines, "First Banana: A Welcome to a New Land," *New York Times Metro Report* (July 31, 1994), 33; Joan Nathan, *Jewish Cooking in America* (New York: Alfred A. Knopf, 1998), 363–64.

32. Samuel C. Prescott, "Consider the Banana," *Good Housekeeping* 65 (October 1917), 79.

33. Samuel C. Prescott, "Banana: A Food of Exceptional Value," *Scientific Monthly* 6 (January 1918), 75.

34. Prescott, "Consider the Banana," 75.

36. B. R. Murphy, "A Cheap Food We Overlook," *Ladies Home Journal* 35 (March 1918), 52.

37. "Cook Your Bananas," *Literary Digest* 56 (February 16, 1918), 22.

38. "From the Tropics to Your Table" (New York: Fruit Dispatch Company, 1926), 26.

39. Home Economics Department, *A Study of the Banana: Its Every-Day Use and Food Value* (New York: United Fruit, 1939), 14.

40. *The Chiquita Banana Cookbook* (Chiquita Brands, New York: Avon Books), 1974.

41. Official Transportation Map, Department of Transportation, Pennsylvania (c. 1993).

42. *Unifruitco* 25:12 (December 29, 1967), 7.

43. "The Banana Split . . . and Does New Things for Your Whole Menu!" *Ladies Home Journal* (April 1976), 120.

44. "What's Cooking across the Country?" *Taste of Home* (1993), 48.

45. Percy Collins, "Quaint Dessert Dishes," *American Homes and Gardens* 8 (February 1911), 57.

46. Elizabeth Schwarts, "The King's Eating Habits Deadly, Expert Says," *Cable News Network* (August 16, 1995).

47. R. H. Stover and N. W. Simmonds, *Bananas* (New York: Longman Scientific and Technical, 1987), 408.

48. Artemis Ward, *The Grocers' Hand-Book and Directory for 1886* (Philadelphia: Philadelphia Grocer Publishing, 1885), 18.

49. "Cider and Vinegar from Bananas," *Literary Digest* 100 (March 16, 1929), 34.

50. Stover and Simmonds, *Bananas*, 396–97.

51. J. A. LeClerc and V. A. Pease, rev. by Harry W. von Loesecke, "Banana Flour as Meal, and Other Commercial Food Products from the Banana: Selected References and Patents Covering Preparation, Uses, Properties," Agricultural Chemical Research Division, Bureau of Agricultural Chemistry and Engineering, Department of Agriculture (typescript, February 27, 1941, and August 27, 1942), 1.

52. "Dried Bananas," *The Cook* 1:7 (May 11, 1885), 7.

53. S. E. Worrell, "Dry Bananas," *Scientific American* 90 (April 16, 1904), 311.

54. Worrell, "Dry Bananas," 311.

55. "Some Facts about Bananas," *Scientific American* 75 (October 10, 1896), 284.

56. "The Bread of the Tropics," *Scientific American* 65 (October 10, 1891), 224.

57. "Some Facts about Bananas," 284.

58. "The Banana as the Basis of a New Industry," *Scientific American* 80 (March 4, 1899), 137.

59. "Banana Flour," *Scientific American Supplement* 50 (August 18, 1900), 20601.

60. "Banana Flour," 20601.

61. "Banana Flour, A New Substitute for Wheat and Rye Flour," *Scientific American* 113 (July 3, 1915), 35.

62. "Banana Flour, A New Substitute for Wheat and Rye Flour," 35.

63. "Banana Flour to Help Fortify America Against a Bread Famine," *Current Opinion* 63 (November 1917), 355.

64. "Possibilities of Dried Bananas," *Literary Digest* 72 (January 7, 1922), 21.

65. "Possibilities of Dried Bananas," 22.

66. "Possibilities of Dried Bananas," 22.

67. Murrill, "The Banana and Its Uses: Getting Acquainted with This Tropical Fruit," 119.

68. "United Fruit Bananas Converted into a New Drink and a Baby Food: Melzo," *Business Week* (October 7, 1933), 10.

69. "United Fruit Bananas Converted into a New Drink and a Baby Food: Melzo," 10.

70. "United Fruit Bananas Converted into a New Drink and a Baby Food: Melzo," 10.

71. "United Fruit Bananas Converted into A New Drink and a Baby Food: Melzo," 10.

72. "Postwar Use for Dried Bananas," *Science Digest* 15 (April 1944), 96.

73. E. D. Stratton, "Bananas: Fruits, Tropical, N.O.S., Dried or Evaporated Fruits," Association of American Railroads, Railroad Committee for the Study of Transportation, Subcommittee on Economic Study Group 4 (typescript, July 24, 1946), viii.

74. M. deG. Bryan and E. Plotz, "Methods of Retarding the Rate of Darkening of Cut Bananas," *Journal of Home Economics* (February 1935), 98.

75. Stover and Simmonds, *Bananas,* 424.

76. Stover and Simmonds, *Bananas,* 398.

77. Stover and Simmonds, *Bananas,* 400.

78. Dean D. Duxbury, "More Banana Variety," *Food Processing* (November 1991), 125.

79. "Hints from Heloise," *Washington Post* (March 10, 1998), D11.

80. Duxbury, "More Banana Variety," 125.

81. Stover and Simmonds, *Bananas,* 398–99.

82. "Bananas, Barbeques and Beverages . . . What's the Story?" *Prepared Foods* (May 1992), 129.

7. CELEBRATING BANANAS

1. "International Banana Festival: Bananas and Good Friends," Fulton, Kentucky, Chamber of Commerce (typescript, 1991), 1.

2. Eighth Annual International Banana Festival Program (Fulton, Kentucky, 1970), 11.

3. Curlin Reed, "Dad's Night," *Saturday Evening Post* (June 30, 1945), 18.

4. Fulton County Historical Society, *Fulton County History* 1 (Dallas: Taylor Publishing, 1983), 20.

5. "Fulton Goes Bananas in a Festive Style," *Commercial Appeal Weekend Living* (Memphis, Tennessee, August 17, 1979).

6. *Fulton County History* 1, 390.

7. Interview with Mary Nelle Wright, Fulton, Kentucky (September 1962).

8. "Fulton Goes Bananas in a Festive Style."

9. "Fulton Goes Bananas in a Festive Style."

10. *Fulton County History* 1, 468.

11. *Fulton County News* (August 19, 1971), 1.

12. Sixth Annual International Banana Festival Program (1968), 35.

13. *Fulton Daily Leader* (September 20, 1982), 2.

14. *Fulton County History* 1, 468.

15. *Fulton Daily Leader,* 2.

16. Sixth Annual International Banana Festival Program, Fulton, Kentucky–South Fulton, Tennessee (September 4–7, 1968), 19.

17. Sixth Annual International Banana Festival Program, 21.

18. Sixth Annual International Banana Festival Program, 13.

19. Jacqueline McGlade, "The U.S. Technical Assistance and Productivity Program and the Education of Western European Managers, 1948–59," in T. R. Gourvish and N. Tiratsoo, *Missionaries and Managers: American Influences on European Management Education, 1945–60* (Manchester University Press, 1997), 13–33.

20. "Thirty Years of Sentiments and Memories," International Banana Festival Program, Chamber of Commerce of the Twin Cities, Fulton, Kentucky (1992), 20; "International Banana Festival: Bananas and Good Friends," 2.

21. Sixth Annual International Banana Festival Program, 33.

22. "Thirty Years of Sentiments and Memories," 21.

23. Sixth Annual International Banana Festival Program, 35.

24. Interview with Paul Westpheling, Fulton, Kentucky, (September, 1992).

25. Sixteenth Annual International Banana Festival Program (1978), 18.

26. Sixth Annual International Banana Festival Program, 19.

27. Sixth Annual International Banana Festival Program, 21; "Thirty Years of Sentiments and Memories," 22.

28. Sixth Annual International Banana Festival Program, 35.

29. Editorial in *Fulton County News* (August 24, 1972), 2.

30. Sixth Annual International Banana Festival Program, 19.

31. Fourteenth Annual International Banana Festival Program (1976), 6.

32. Eighth Annual International Banana Festival Program, 35, 37.

33. Eighth Annual International Banana Festival Program, 17.

34. Eighth Annual International Banana Festival Program, 15.

35. *Fulton Daily Leader* (September 20, 1982), 10.

36. "International Banana Festival: Bananas and Good Friends," 2.

37. Twenty-fifth Annual International Banana Festival Program (Fulton, Kentucky, 1987), 7.

38. Sixth Annual International Banana Festival Program, 31.

39. Eighth Annual International Banana Festival Program, 19.

40. Fourteenth Annual International Banana Festival Program, 38.

41. Sixth Annual International Banana Festival Program, 29.

42. Sixth Annual International Banana Festival Program, 27.

43. Eighth Annual International Banana Festival Program, 15.

44. Eighth Annual International Banana Festival Program, 15.

45. Eighth Annual International Banana Festival Program, 17.

46. Twenty-sixth Annual International Banana Festival Program (Fulton, Kentucky, 1988), 12.

47. *Fulton County History* 1, 21.

48. "Jo's Notebook," *Fulton County News* (August 24, 1972), 8.

49. Twenty-fifth Annual International Banana Festival Program, 19.

50. Interview with Mary Nelle Wright, Fulton, Kentucky, (September 1992).

51. Thirtieth Annual International Banana Festival Program (Fulton, Kentucky, 1992), 47.

8. MEANING OF BANANAS

1. Sidney W. Mintz, *Sweetness and Power: The Place of Sugar in Modern History* (New York: Elizabeth Seaton Books/Viking, 1985).

2. Quaker Oats Company, *Woman's Home Companion* (March 1910), 58; "Shredded Ralston," *American Magazine* (November 1939), 143.

3. Kraft General Foods, Post Banana Nut Crunch, (Introductory store coupon, 1993).

4. B. Roueche, "The Humblest Fruit," *New Yorker* 49 (October 1, 1973), 48.

5. David Widner, "America's Going Bananas," *Reader's Digest* (July 1986), 118.

6. *New York Times* (March 8, 1993), D8.

7. Personal communication from Gene Murrow (February 5, 1992).

8. Martin V. Melosi, *Garbage in the Cities: Refuse, Reform, and the Environment, 1880–1980* (College Station: Texas A&M University Press, 1981), 67, 74.

9. Francis Forrester, "Mind Where You Throw Orange Peel," *Sunday School Advocate* 20:23 (September 14, 1861), 89–90.

10. Edith E. Wiggin, *Lessons on Manners for School and Home Use* (Boston: Lee and Shepard, 1884), 23.

11. *Harper's Weekly* (April 26, 1879), 331.

12. *The Cook* 1:19 (August 3, 1885), 11.

13. George A. Soper, *Modern Methods of Street Cleaning* (New York: Engineering News Publishing, 1909), 8.

14. Report of a Committee of the New York Municipal Society Appointed to Investigate the System of Street Cleaning as Administered by the Board of Police of the City of New York (New York: 1878).

15. William A. Richmann, *The Sweep of Time* (Elgin, Illinois: Elgin Sweeper Company, 1962), 28.

16. George E. Waring Jr., *Street Cleaning* (New York: Doubleday and McClure, 1898), 183; Melosi, *Garbage in the Cities: Refuse, Reform, and the Environment, 1880–1980*, 75.

17. Waring, *Street Cleaning*, 181.

18. Waring, *Street Cleaning*, 182.

19. Waring, *Street Cleaning*, 184.

20. Department of Street Cleaning, City of New York, *Report for Year 1909*, 11.

21. *Annual Report of Department of Street Cleaning for the Year 1912* (New York, N.Y.), 3.

22. Melosi, *Garbage in The Cities: Refuse, Reform, and the Environment, 1880–1980*, 76.

23. Civic Improvement League, *Keep Our City Clean* (Saint Louis: C. P. Curran, 1902), 12.

24. *Harper's Weekly* (May 29, 1880), 343.

25. John Wilcock, "About: Bananas," *New York Times Magazine* (March 30, 1958), 53.

26. Wilcock, "About: Bananas," 53.

27. "Joey Faye," *The Economist* (May 10, 1997), 88.

28. *Drummer's Yarns or Fun on the "Road"* (New York: Excelsior Publishing House, 1886), 71.

29. *The Smile on the Face of the Tiger: A Collection of Limericks* (Boston: Bacon and Brown, 1910); Clement Wood, ed., *A Book of Humorous Limericks* (Little Blue Book 1018, Girard, Kansas: Huldeman-Julius Company), 1926.

30. Michael Neve, "Freud's Theory of Humor, Wit and Jokes," in *Laughing Matters: A Serious Look at Humor* (New York: Longman Scientific and Technical, 1998), 40.

31. Jonathan Miller, "Jokes and Joking: A Serious Laughing Matter," in *Laughing Matters: A Serious Look at Humor* (New York: Longman Scientific and Technical, 1988), 10.

32. Frank J. MacHovec, *Humor: Theory, History, Applications* (Springfield, Illinois: Charles C. Thomas, 1988), 54.

33. Quoted in Neve, "Freud's Theory of Humor, Wit and Jokes," 36.

34. *Harper's Weekly* (July 27, 1878), 591.

35. Raymond Sokolov, "Bananamania," *Natural History* (May 1977), 80.

36. *Unifruitco* 24:10 (United Fruit, October 31, 1966), 7.

37. MacHovec, *Humor: Theory, History, Applications,* 67.

38. MacHovec, *Humor: Theory, History, Applications,* 67.

39. Stephen Leacock, *Humor: Its Theory and Technique* (New York: Dodd Mead, 1935), 11.

40. Roueche, "The Humblest Fruit," 48.

41. William Breisky, "But Yes, We Had Bananas—Coming Out of Our Ears," *Smithsonian* (March 1977), 101.

42. *Justice* 75:6 (New York: International Ladies' Garment Workers' Union, September 1993), 20.

43. Leacock, *Humor: Its Theory and Technique,* 201.

44. Marina Warner, *No Go the Bogeyman: Scaring, Lulling, and Making Mock* (New York: Farrar, Straus and Giroux, 1998), 372.

45. Kirk Varnedoe and Adam Gopnik, *High and Low: Modern Art and Popular Culture* (Museum of Modern Art, New York: Harry N. Abrams, 1990).

46. "Hagar the Horrible" by Chris Browne, *Washington Post,* (April 12, 1992); "The Fusco Brothers" by J. C. Duffy, *Washington Post* (July 15, 1992); Gary Larson, *Washington Post* (August 7, 1994); "Mother Goose & Grimm" by Mike Peters, *Washington Post* (February 18, 1995); "Speed Bump" by Dave Coverly, *Washington Post* (July 26, 1995); "BC" by Hart, *Washington Post* (August 27, 1995, and October 31, 1997); "Garfield" by Jim Davis, *Washington Post* (May 26, 1996); "Broom Hilda" by Russell Myers, *Washington Post* (May 23, 1997, and January 15, 1998); "Beetle Bailey" by Mort Walker, *Washington Post* (January 24, 1998); "Ralph" by Wayne Stayskal, *Washington Post* (February 22, 1998).

47. Debra Barracca and Sal Barracca, *Maxi the Hero* (New York: Dial Books for Young Readers, 1992).

48. Thomas C. Mann and Janet Greene, *Sudden and Awful: American Epitaphs and the Finger of God* (Brattleboro: Stephen Greene Press, 1968), 28.

49. Alex Abella, *The Total Banana and the Illustrated Banana: Anecdotes, History, Recipes and More!* (New York: Harcourt Brace Jovanovich, 1979), 30.

50. Ken Dornstein, *Accidentally, On Purpose: The Making of a Personal Injury Underworld in America* (St. Martin's Press, 1996; review in *Washington Post Book World* [February 16, 1997, 6]).

51. Copy of 1950s' brochure and recollection provided by Jane Webb Smith.

52. Robert Clyde Allen, *Vaudeville and Film, 1895–1915: A Study in Media Interaction* (New York: Arno Press, 1980), 83, 123, 126.

53. Recollections of Valarie Brown, Department of American Studies, University of Maryland at College Park, January 14, 1998, and Nancy C. Van Den Akker, New Orleans Public Library, January 13, 1998.

54. Widner, "America's Going Bananas," 117; Wilcock, "About: Bananas," 53.

55. Abella, *The Total Banana and the Illustrated Banana: Anecdotes, History, Recipes and More!* 30.

56. MacHovec, *Humor: Theory, History, Applications,* 4.

57. MacHovec, *Humor: Theory, History, Applications,* 44.

58. William Safire, "On Language," in *New York Times Magazine* (May 9, 1993).

59. Abella, *The Total Banana and the Illustrated Banana,* 31.

60. Marina Warner, *No Go the Bogeyman: Scaring, Lulling, and Making Mock* (New York: Farrar, Straus and Giroux, 1998), 368.

61. Warner, *No Go the Bogeyman: Scaring, Lulling, and Making Mock,* 367.

62. Sokolov, "Bananamania," 81.

63. *The Cook* 1:14 (June 19, 1885), 12.

64. James Ellis Humphrey, "Where Bananas Grow," *Popular Science* (February 1894), 486.

65. C. B. Hayward, "Culture and Transportation," *Scientific American* (January 28, 1905), 80.

66. Ralph W. Dexter, "Tarantula in Captivity," *Nature Magazine* (May 1946), 229.

67. Waverly Root and Richard de Rochemont, *Eating in America: A History* (New York: William Morrow, 1976), 235.

68. February 28, 1993.

69. August 28, 1991.

70. Marilyn Vos Savant, "Ask Marilyn," *Parade Magazine* (September 26, 1993), 18.

71. Don Cusic, "Comedy and Humor in Country Music," *Journal of American Culture* (Summer 1993), 49.

72. Robert L. Chapman, ed., *New Dictionary of American Slang* (New York: Harper and Row, 1986), 170.

73. "B.C." by Hart, *Washington Post* (December 13, 1997).

74. "That's Life" by Mike Twohy, *Washington Post* (April 15, 1999), C12.

75. "Ernie" by Bud Grade, *Washington Post* (October 12, 1994).

76. "Dennis the Menace" by Hank Ketcham, *Washington Post* (May 19, 1996).

77. *Washington Post Weekend* (August 8, 1977), 41.

78. With thanks to Ann Lovell, curator of the Banana Museum, Auburn, Washington.

79. Neve, "Freud's Theory of Humor, Wit and Jokes," 37.

80. "Mellow Yellow," *Newsweek* (April 10, 1967), 93.

81. "Yes, They Sell More Bananas," *Business Week* (July 8, 1967), 92.

82. "Tripping on Banana Peels," *Time* (April 7, 1967), 52.

83. "Mellow Yellow," 93.

84. "Yes, They Sell More Bananas," 92; "The Big Banana Hoax," *Science Digest* (February 1968), 63.

85. "Tripping on Banana Peels," 52.

86. "Mellow Yellow," 93.

87. "Yes, They Sell More Bananas," 92.

88. *The Workbasket: Home and Needlecraft for Pleasure and Profit* 16:4 (January 1952), 73.

89. *Unifruitco* 24:9 (September 30, 1966), 3.

90. *The American Traveler* (American Airlines, Summer 1992), 3.

91. John Kaiser, "Auburn Collector Will Help National TV Show Go Bananas," *Valley Daily News* (July 7, 1995), A1.

92. Paula Borchardt, *Sky Magazine* (February 1995), 15.

93. "Ken Bannister Isn't Just One of the Bunch When He Slips into His Favorite Banana Suit," *People* (November 12, 1984), 84.

94. Mintz, *Sweetness and Power: The Place of Sugar in Modern History,* 120.

INDEX